No Exit Necessary: Reno, NV to Adelanto, CA

US 395 Series

J. Butler Kyle

Published by Nomad Publications NV, 2022.

Table of Contents

Nevada Facts and Trivia 1

Washoe County, Nevada 5

Carson City, Nevada 19

Douglas County, Nevada 25

California Facts and Trivia 43

Mono County, California 45

Inyo County, California 73

Kern County, California 101

San Bernardino County, California 107

Alternate/Old US 395 Southbound 113

Alternate/Old US 395 Northbound 121

US 395 Business Route (Carson City) Southbound 129

US 395 Business Route (Carson City) Northbound 133

Index | Nevada Index 137

Nevada Index of Attractions 139

Nevada Index of Camping and Day Use Parks 141

Nevada Index of Cities 143

Nevada Index of Counties 145

Nevada Index of Historical Markers and Monuments 147

Nevada Index of Lakes, Rivers, and Water Sheds 149

Nevada Index of Mountains and Summits 151

Nevada Index of Ranger Stations 153

Nevada Index of Native American Information 155

Nevada Index of Roads 157

California Index 159

California Index of Attractions 161

California Index of Camping and Day Use Parks 163

California Index of Cities 165

California Index of Counties 167

California Index of Deserts, Mountains, and Summits 169

California Index of Historical Markers and Monuments 171

California Index of Lakes, Rivers, and Reservoirs 173

California Index of National Forest and Wilderness, and Ranger Stations .. 175

California Index of Native American Information 177

California Index of Rest Areas 179

California Index of Roads 181

Index of QR Codes for Websites and Other Links 183

References 197

To my husband Bill, thanks for the many, *many* miles.

Although, elaboration on "Bag" would have been appreciated.

"Wander often. Wonder always." *Anonymous*

Copyright © 2022 by J. Butler Kyle

All rights reserved.

The scanning, uploading, and distribution of this book without permission is a theft of the author's intellectual property. If you would like permission to use material from the book (other than for review purposes), please contact the publisher at nomadpublicationsnv@yahoo.com

The author asserts the moral right to be identified as the author of this work.

The author has no responsibility for the accuracy of websites or URLs for external or third-party Internet Websites referred to in this publication, and does not guarantee that any content on such Websites is, or will remain, accurate or appropriate.

Designations used by companies to distinguish their products are often claimed as trademarks. All brand names and product names used in this book and on its cover are trade names, service marks, trademarks, and registered trademarks of their respective owners. The publishers and the book are not associated with any product or vendor mentioned in this book. However, it is possible some companies referenced within have endorsed this book.

First Printing, 2022

ISBN EPUB 979-8-9869686-0-5

ISBN PRINT 979-8-9869686-1-2

Nomad Publications NV, Wellington, NV 89444

nomadpublicationsnv@yahoo.com

Cover art designed by Heidi Thompson, *Bristlecone Studios*

Preface

Through the years, as Bill and I motored around the country, we've always liked pouring over a map of the area we're traveling through. When we were going back and forth to Alaska, *The Milepost* was our favorite book to take along. If you have ever used it, you know what I mean, and I'm sure you'll agree. In that spirit, that's how this book came about. It is a mile-by-mile companion, travel guide filled with things to see and do along the way, bits of history and trivia, inscriptions on Historic markers and monuments, links to interesting and fun stories, as well as helpful notes you might need to be aware of that could make your trip go smoother (such as where is the next electric-vehicle charging station). It is purely entertainment to make some of those long miles go quicker. *JBK*

Acknowledgment

So many folks helped in the making of this travel companion, some of them without even knowing it.

To those special few:

Thank you Bill Kyle, for pointing things out I wasn't muttering about at the time. Your unintended participation is always welcome.

To my *favorite* minions- Jack Butler, you are the best brother, and Terri Fahey, a most special sis. You two have my gratitude for your enthusiasm and encouragement. Also, a specially whoohoo for taking the time to drive each mile with me. It was *fun*. Jack, your dedication to trying each link and website makes this entertaining trip trivia *remarkable*.

To these ladies and fine gentlemen- Janeanne Ward, Ross and Evanna Judkins, Allison Melton, Deb Rothchild, Lauren Saunders, Susan Saunders, and Val & Kim Straw, I cannot thank you enough for so graciously listening, for your terrific suggestions, and those gentle persuasions when I veered off yonder. Especially *Thank You* for being such good friends. Ross, your eagle eye kept me from looking like an idiot.

Jamie, Anthony, Ajax, and Tara at Draft2Digital, when you said we could, I was walking on air! Here's to a fine future together.

Joe, Bishop Chamber of Commerce, your knowledge of Inyo County and surrounding area, and willingness to share with me was so appreciated and just a delight to listen to. Offering me your time made this book so much more special. Thank you!

Special thanks to the following folk for taking the time to answer so many questions. Your help was invaluable and so appreciated: Lynda, Bridgeport Chamber of Commerce; Nick, Mono County Board of Supervisors; Barbara, Mono Lake Tufa Natural Reserve; and Kendra, library@dot.ca.gov.

For permission to include the wording of their monuments, thank you to the various E Clampus Vitus Chapters, this input made the book so much more interesting – Snowshoe Thomson Chapter #1827, Bodie Chapter #64, Slim Princess Chapter #395, and Billy Holcomb #1069

Introduction

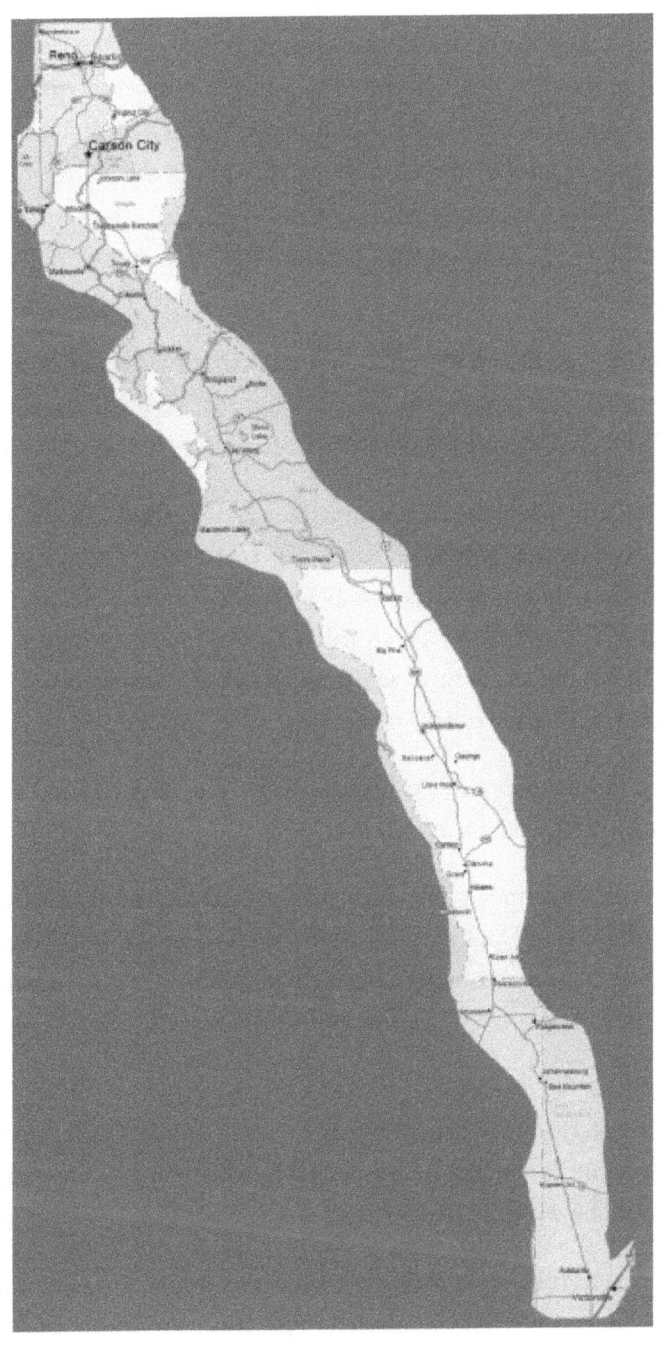

This mile-by-mile roadside attraction and travel companion of US Highway 395 begins at the Nevada/California line at Bordertown, Nevada, and continues southbound to its terminus at I-15 in Adelanto, California. It is filled with trivia and information of all sorts to help you enjoy your travels. This print version has QR Codes and a couple of web addresses in the Index for external links to various websites. **Note:** *Scanning these QR Codes will take you to the internet.* <u>Please keep in mind that we cannot guarantee the accuracy or timeliness of the information on these websites,</u> **nor their security**, <u>so use with care and caution.</u>

How to use this guide: Each entry begins with a Milepost or Mile Marker followed by what that entry is about. For example, **WA 40: A:** would mean at Milepost Washoe County 40 is an Attraction. Below are the entry explanations.

Milepost or Mile Marker: These are the vertical signs on the edge of the road that are placed at one-mile intervals. In both Nevada and California, they denote the county abbreviation as well as the mile (For example WA 07 would mean Washoe County seven miles north or east of where you crossed the county line.) The mile starts at the southern or western point on the road and increases as you drive north or east.

In this Travel Guide each entry is listed in bold (e.g., **WA 07**) and will be *at* the Milepost or Mile Marker, or *within* that mile.

Warning: It doesn't mean it's dire, just something to take notice of. For example, it might be a Daylight Headlight Section and headlights are required to be on. It is also used to forewarn of steep grades both up and down. However, if a percentage is not listed, then there is no specific sign along the road telling what the percentage is.

Note: When you see this word, this may be some thought that popped into my brain or I thought you might be interested in whatever it points out, or simply that you should be aware of something.

For example, did you know Adopt-A-Highway began in 1985 after a Texas Department of Transportation engineer saw trash fly from a pickup truck. A group of volunteers 'adopted' a two-mile section of road to keep clean. Today, organizations that adopt a section of road are allowed to have their names displayed on a sign. Sponsor-A-Highway allows the organization to have its name on the sign but they pay for professional contractors to do the work.

Look: This indicates something caught my eye and I thought you would like to see it. It will be within the next mile and point out which direction to look – NORTH, SOUTH, EAST, WEST; possibly right or left. (If you are new to compass points, Southbound finds West to the right, and East to the left. Conversely, Northbound sees West to the left and East to the right.)

RA: Rest Area. (Thank you to the Maintenance Crews that work hard to keep the Rest Areas clean!)

NA: This is information on Native American Tribes or the Reservation.

Camping: These campgrounds are either Federal, State, or County. Of course, there are also private campgrounds, but those are not listed. The only information provided is how to google the campground, otherwise, nothing specific is noted about it.

A: This means there is an **attraction** of some sort, such as a Historic Marker, monument, vista site, or point of interest. Keep in mind it will be within the next mile.

Historic markers and monuments that you pass along the way all have the words written here so if you don't have time to stop, you can still read what it says. The passage will be indented to denote it is a transcript of the monument. These monuments are transcribed verbatim as the plaque reads, with misspellings and punctuation included.

If you see something you would expect to find information on and there isn't any, it's either because I couldn't find anything on it or haven't noticed it myself. Let me know and I will include it, if possible, in the next edition with an acknowledgment of your contribution. Please send two photos – 1) that shows an overview of the area; 2) that clearly shows the sight or words and who created the sign or monument. You can send them to: jbutlerkyle@yahoo.com

Disclaimer: *In no way* should this book be considered or construed as advice or a recommendation. Also, please be aware mileage may be out of order if it's not pertinent to the drive or interferes with the flow of information. And last, mileage is as close as possible but it *can* be off.

In construction zones, detours happen and roads change. Do not rely on this guide for accurate, up-to-date information. As always, obey construction and hazard signs.

Between editions, you can go to the website: jbutlerkyle.com[1] to sign up for updates on attractions, other news, or changing information.

As with all road trips, obey the laws, follow the signs, don't always rely on your GPS, be safe, and most of all enjoy your travels.

As Ralph Waldo Emerson wrote and Aerosmith implied:

"It's not the destination, it's the journey."

---

1. https://jbutlerkyle.com/

Nevada Facts and Trivia

Nevada gained Statehood on October 31, 1864. It is the 36th state. Nevada is the 7th-most extensive in size and the 19th-least populated of the US states. It is bordered by five states- Oregon, Idaho, California, Utah, and Arizona. Las Vegas is home to three-quarters of the state's population, with Reno second. There are sixteen counties in the state. The smallest is Esmeralda County, near the center of the state, and is the least populated with under a thousand people. Clark County, where Las Vegas is, is the most populated with over 2,000,000 people. Locals pronounce the name as 'Nevădă' (as in ăpple). The name 'Nevada' comes from the Spanish word of the same spelling, meaning 'snow-covered,' after the snow on the Sierra Nevada mountains. Carson City is the state capital.

State Nicknames:

The Silver State because of the Comstock Lode. In 1877, at peak production, the mines produced over $14,000,000 of gold and $21,000,000 of silver that year. (At current value that would be about $340,243,750 and $510,365, 625.)

The state is also called The Battle Born State as it was granted statehood during the Civil War.

Because of the abundance of the state flower, Nevada is also called The Sagebrush State.

Nevada State Symbols:

- Flower: Sagebrush
- Bird: Mountain Bluebird
- Animal: Desert Bighorn Sheep
- Colors: Silver and Blue
- Metal: Silver
- Fossil: Ichthyosaur

J. BUTLER KYLE

<u>Nevada Trivia</u>:

- Samuel Clemens, aka Mark Twain, worked as a reporter in Virginia City in 1862.
- Gambling was legalized in 1931.
- In Death Valley, the Kangaroo Rat can live its entire life without drinking a drop of liquid.
- Nevada has more mountain ranges than any other state.
- Hoover Dam has enough concrete, 3.25 million cubic yards, to pave a two-lane highway from San Francisco to New York.
- Camels were used as pack animals as late as 1870.
- Tonopah had at least two famous residents – Wyatt Earp, lawman and folk hero, who was a US Marshall for a short time; and boxer Jack Dempsey tended bar and acted as bouncer at the Mispah Hotel and Casino.
- Nevada ranks fourth in top gold production in the world and seventy-eight percent of the United States.

NO EXIT NECESSARY: RENO, NV TO ADELANTO, CA

Washoe County, Nevada

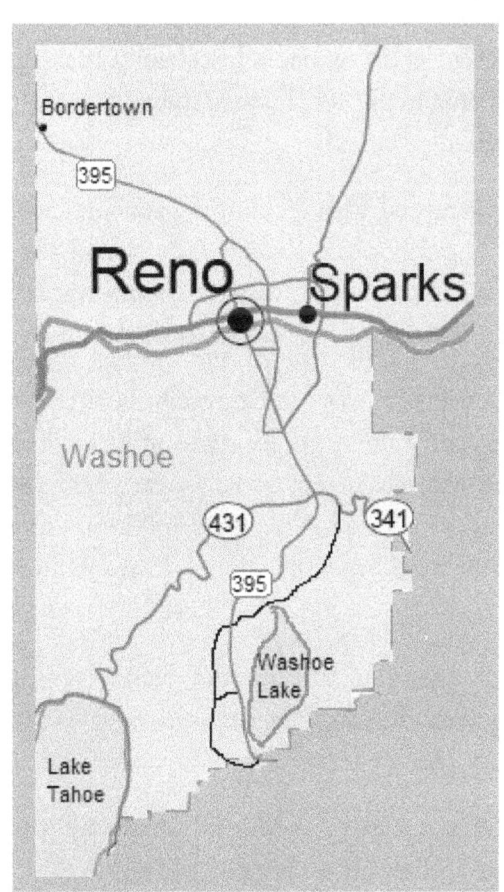

WA 41: Washoe County [Milepost Sign designated as **WA**] has a population of about 486,000. At 6,600 square miles, it is a little larger than the state of Massachusetts. US 395 travels 41 miles through Washoe County. Reno is the county seat.

A small group of Bannock Indians under a leader named "Shoshone Mike" killed four ranchers in Washoe County. A posse was formed, and on February 26, 1911, they caught up with the band, and eight of them were killed, along with one of the posse, Ed Hogle. Three children and a woman who survived the battle were captured. The remains of some of the members of the band were repatriated from the Smithsonian Institution to Fort Hall, Idaho, Shoshone-Bannock Tribe in 1994.

In 1918, Washoe County elected Sadie Hurst, a Republican, to the Nevada Legislature. She was the first woman ever elected to that political body. In 2018, one hundred years later, for the first time in Nevada history, there were more than fifty percent women in the Legislature.

For decades the federal government required Paiute children growing up in northern Nevada to attend a boarding school in Carson City where they learned English, not their native Paiute. As of 2013, Washoe County was the first school district in the state to offer Paiute language classes as an elective.

Follow **US Highway 395 (US 395)**, a South/North route through the Western United States. It is 1,305 miles long and came into existence in 1926. The southern end of the route is in the Mojave Desert at I-15 near Hesperia, California. The northern terminus is at the Canada–US border in Washington. Originally the route went all the way to San Diego, but when I-15 was built it replaced that stretch of road.

In Nevada and California, US 395 runs along the Eastern Sierra Nevada beginning at Border Town/Cold Springs. It tops four summits over 7,000', continues down through Owens Valley, and then crosses the Mojave Desert.

This section of highway, through Reno, is known as Martin Luther King Jr. Highway. It is also part of the Sponsor-a-Highway program.

WA 41: Although **Bordertown** is the very first exit in Nevada (exit 83), it had no town or census designation of its own. It is in conjunction with the community of Cold Springs. Border Town is best known for the casino there.

WA 41: California Trail crossing: Although the California Trail has no official road marker near Bordertown, it is the first of three major routes to California here in Nevada. This route would take the pioneers and gold seekers north, up what is known today as the Upper Long Valley, where they would

NO EXIT NECESSARY: RENO, NV TO ADELANTO, CA

turn west into California near present-day Hallelujah Junction and further westbound on the present-day CA 70 corridor past Quincy, California.

The California Trail brought more than 200,000 people seeking a new life during the 1840s and 1850s. The 2,400-mile trail was one of many wagon roads and footpaths traveling westward. In all, four routes left Omaha and Nebraska City, Nebraska; and St. Joseph and Kansas City, Missouri, coming together more or less near present-day Kearney, Nebraska. The trail continued along near present-day I-80 until around Ogallala, Nebraska. From there, the trail veered northwest up toward present-day Casper, Wyoming. Near the southern end of the Wind River Range, the trails split apart into several different routes venturing as far north as present-day Pocatello, Idaho, and as far south as Salt Lake City, Utah. The many trails came together near present-day Elko, Nevada, and ran along the I-80 corridor to Lovelock, Nevada, where the trail forked, traveling south toward present-day Reno and Carson City, or north into the Black Rock Desert. This section was particularly treacherous and was known as the Forty Mile Desert, where if any water was found, it was unusable.

To see an interactive map, *scan the QR Code in the Index of Websites:* **California Trail Crossing**. On the left side of the screen are the various trail layers. This is where you can unclick as many trails as you want. The California Trail is indicated by the green line.

WA 40: Warning: Uphill grade next two miles.

WA 39: Cold Springs Valley is a bedroom community of Reno with a population of about 8,500.

WA 39: Warning: Downhill grade next two miles.

WA 39: A: Exit 78. **Sierra Nevada Zoological Park** (WEST) is on N Virginia Street. **Animal Ark** (EAST) wildlife park is twelve miles out Red Rock Road.

Nevada Historic Transportation marker #256 **"Historic Transportation"** (WEST) is in the parking lot immediately on the corner of N Virginia Street on a large granite boulder. The sun has faded many of the words, but what is visible reads:

J. BUTLER KYLE

"Historic Transportation From Honey Lake to Virginia City

The historic road corridor from the Truckee Meadows northwestward into the Honey Lake area contains a tangle of intertwined routes *(missing words)* of valleys, portions of an immigrant trail cutoff, toll roads, county roads, and casual parallel routes developed to bypass blocked *(missing words)*. Construction of the paved precursor to US 395 and recent freeway construction along this same corridor have *(missing words)* system cutting it into isolated segments. The road is associated with the continuing history of transportation in the state of Nevada *(missing words)* process of road improvement and economic and demographic change.

Highway System 1930s to Present

The Three Flags Highway gave way to US 395 which was an extension of Virginia Street in Reno. In the 1970s a 4-lane system was proposed. The highway generally follows the same transportation corridor and still cuts through the Peavine Ranch Property.

Three Flags Highway 1923-1950s

One of the first Federally funded highways in Nevada was *(missing words)* from Reno to the Nevada/California border. The Nevada highway *(missing words)* was organized in 1917, federal money was mandated for Nevada in 1921 and construction started in April 1922 for the Three Flags Highway the road linking Canada, the United States, and Mexico. Portions of the road still remain.

Toll Roads 1850s-1860s

Prior to State and Federally constructed highways a *(missing words)* a stage and toll road between Honey Lake and Virginia City was more or less maintained under a succession of private owners such as Myron C. Lake. In 1861, Lake traded property in Honey Lake

NO EXIT NECESSARY: RENO, NV TO ADELANTO, CA

Valley for the log toll bridge across the Truckee River with Charles W. Fuller of Susanville. Lake applied for a franchise to improve, maintain, and construct a toll road from three miles south of this bridge (Exit 78) to the California/Nevada border excluding passage through towns, streets of Reno. The early road, approximately twenty miles long, *(missing words)* deplorable condition and impassable at times.

This marker is placed through the cooperation of the Sierra Pacific Power Company, Nevada Department of Transportation, State Historic Preservation Office and United States Bureau of Land Management."

Note: At the time of this publishing, the author had reached out to the Department of Transportation and State Historic Preservation Office, for the full text, but had not received a response.

WA 34: Stead (Exit 76) is another bedroom community of Reno. It is most famous for its Reno Air Races. The Reno-Stead Airport is a large public and military general aviation airport.

It was a military installation from 1942-1966 when it was known as Stead Air Force Base and was primarily used for survival training by the Strategic Air Command. The airport's remaining military presence is an Army Aviation Support Facility and the 189th General Support Aviation Battalion of the Nevada Army National Guard. They fly CH-47 Chinook helicopters.

Although most US airports use the same three-letter location identifier for the FAA (Federal Aviation Administration) as well as IATA (International Air Transport Association). Stead is assigned RTS (formerly 4SD) by the FAA but doesn't have an IATA designation. That's because RTS is assigned to Rottnest Island Airport in Rottnest Island, Western Australia.

The airport is also used by the Bureau of Land Management (BLM) as an Air Tanker Base for fire-fighting aircraft. Each fire season two SEATs (Single Engine Air Tankers) are based there and an Air Attack aircraft, but the facility supports S-2s from California as well as the BAEs, RJ-135s, C-130s, and MD-87s.

In the late 1960s, Reno-Stead Airport was operated by Ag Aviation Academy which was owned by the Lear organization. Students were housed in the former married quarters of the Air Force Base. Since 1964, it has been home to the National Championship Air Races, also known as the Reno Air Races, held every September. In the early 1990s, it was the launch site of "Earthwinds" balloon system, which attempted (and failed) multiple times to circumnavigate the globe.

WA 32 Lemmon Valley (Exit 74) is a bedroom community of Reno with a population of around 5,000.

WA 31: Golden Valley (Exit 73) is yet another bedroom community of Reno. Their population is around 1,500. Golden Valley Road is.

Note: The sign indicates "Reno Next 5 Exits." However, there are more than that. The following is a list of the Exit numbers and correlating streets through Reno:

Exit 72 – Business US 395 Loop to Reno is an Exit Only Lane. This offramp is also to Panther Valley.

Exit 71 – Parr Blvd (WEST). The Sheriff's office is this exit.

Exit 71 – Dandini Blvd (EAST). **A: Desert Research Institute** and **Countess Angela Dandini Gardens** are both this direction.

Warning: Begin 6% downgrade. Watch for slow vehicles. **Note:** For Road Information Tune Radio to 580 AM.

Exit 70 – Clear Acre Lane and N McCarran Blvd. This offramp is to Sun Valley also. **Warning:** Offramp is 7% downgrade.

Exit 69 – Oddie Blvd. **Warning:** In 2021 construction begins here, the speed limit was 45 mph.

NO EXIT NECESSARY: RENO, NV TO ADELANTO, CA

Exit 68 – Exit Only lane to I-80 (EAST/WEST) Elko and Sparks (left lane), Sacramento and Downtown Reno (right lane).

Interstate 580 (I-580) merges with US 395. It is an Interstate Highway that runs concurrently with US 395 from I-80 in Reno, at what is locally known as "The Spaghetti Bowl", to US 50 in Carson City. Planning began in 1956 for I-580 but wasn't designated until the 1970s. It was signed as US 395 until 2012 when the road was completed between Reno and Carson City.

Within the Reno city limits, the freeway is designated the Martin Luther King Jr. freeway. Through Carson City, the freeway is designated the Carson City Deputy Sheriff Carl Howell Memorial Freeway in honor of a sheriff's officer who was fatally shot while attempting to rescue a victim of domestic violence from their house.

Note: Throughout Reno, there are 209 various Electric Vehicle charging stations. *Scan the QR Code in the Index:* **EV Stations - RENO** for a link to a map of their locations.

WA 24: Reno is known as "The Biggest Little City in the World." The population is around 241,000. It is the third largest city in the state after Las Vegas and Henderson.

Situated just east of the Sierra Nevada in the high desert on the western edge of the Great Basin, Reno sits about 4,400' above sea level. Approximately twenty-two miles east of Lake Tahoe, the Truckee River runs out of the lake and through downtown on its way to Pyramid Lake.

Geologically, numerous faults exist throughout the region. Most of these are vertical motion faults associated with the uplift of the various mountain ranges, including the Sierra Nevada. In February 2008, an earthquake swarm of nearly 250 temblors began, lasting for several months. The largest quake registered 4.9 on the Richter scale, although some geologic estimates put it at 5.0. The earthquakes were centered in the Somersett community in west Reno near the areas of Mogul and Verdi. Many of the homes in that area were damaged.

Historically, gold was discovered near Virginia City in 1850, and a modest mining community developed, but it was the discovery of silver in 1859 at the Comstock Lode that led to a mining rush. Charles W. Fuller built a log toll bridge across the Truckee River in 1859 to connect Virginia City with the California Trail. A small community that serviced travelers soon grew up near the bridge. After two years, Fuller sold the bridge to Myron C. Lake, who continued to develop the community with the addition of a grist mill, kiln, and livery stable as well as hotel and eating house. He renamed it "Lake's Crossing." In 1864, Washoe County was consolidated with Roop County, and Lake's Crossing became the largest town in the county. Lake earned himself the title "founder of Reno." But it wasn't until May 1868, when the Central Pacific Rail Road built a station that the town was officially named Reno.

WA 22: California Trail crossing: The California Trail has no official road marker through Reno, the second of three major routes to California here in Nevada occurred somewhere around The Spaghetti Bowl, perhaps near Plumb Lane. This route took the pioneers and gold seekers directly west into California along the present-day I-80 corridor. This is the route the doomed Donner Party traveled.

To see an interactive map, *scan the QR Code in the Index of Websites* **California Trail crossing**. On the left side of the screen are the various trail layers. This is where you can unclick as many trails as you want. The California Trail is indicated by the green line.

Note: If you look around the valley to the foothills, you may notice large letters on the side of the hills. These are known as "mountain monograms." They are mostly found in the western states. The first known building of the monogram was in 1905. Here in the Truckee Meadows, the R is for Reno High School, N is University of Nevada, S is Sparks High School, D is Damonte Ranch High School, and G is Galena High School.

Note: This is a continuation of the Exits and correlating streets through Reno:

Exit 35 – E 2nd Street, an Exit Only lane.

Exit 34 – Mill Street. To go to the Hospital, turn right on Mill Street.

NO EXIT NECESSARY: RENO, NV TO ADELANTO, CA

Exit 33B – Reno-Tahoe International Airport. For Airport information tune radio to 1610 AM.

Exit 33A – Plumb Lane and Villanova Drive. **Warning:** Speed limit 65 mph.

Exit 32 – Moana Lane, and to Convention Center.

Exit 31 – South Virginia Street (right). Kietzke Lane (left).

Exit 30 – Neil Road and Meadowwood Mall Way (left). Del Monte Lane (right).

Exit 29 – South Virginia Street.

Exit 28 – South Meadows Parkway.

Exit 26 – Damonte Ranch Parkway, this is an Exit Only lane.

Exit 25B – South Virginia Street. To Virginia City (National Historic Landmark via SR 341.) To N Lake Tahoe (via Mt. Rose Highway/SR 431). To Alternate/Old US 395 Southbound. For a log of this route go to page 103.

Exit 25A – South Virginia Street N.

Warning: Heed the electronic traffic sign if it is warning of winds in Washoe Valley. They can be strong enough to tip over semi-trucks. For Washoe Valley Wind Alert Tune Radio to 580 AM.

WA 13: Exit 24 – **State Route 431** climbs to Mount Rose Summit, 8,911', and into Incline Village or Kings Beach, and Lake Tahoe. This is the highest summit in the Sierra Nevada that is open year-round. Old US 395 and Virginia City can also be reached via this exit.

Warning: Speed limit 70 mph.

WA 13: Did you notice the geothermal plants? These are part of the Steamboat Geothermal Power Complex.

WA 10: The **Galena Creek Bridge** is the world's longest cathedral arch bridge. It is 1,722' long, and the span of the arch is 689'. For an interesting article on the claim, *scan the QR Code in the Index of Websites*: **Galena Creek Bridge** and read Mark Robison's story.

WA 10: Look: Straight south you can see Mt. Rose Ski Area and the antenna of Mount Rose Weather Observatory.

Mt. Rose-Ski Tahoe is 1,300 acres of groomed ski runs. Despite the name, the ski area is actually on the slopes of Slide Mountain rather than Mount Rose. At 8,260', the average yearly snowfall is 30'. But in 2017, a record 761" (63' 5") fell, that's more than double the average at nearly 64' of snow!

"Mount Rose Weather Observatory" is the location of Nevada State Historical Marker #230. It is the highest marker in the state at 8,900'. The marker explains the story best:

> "Two miles to the northwest of this point lies Mt. Rose. On the 10,778 foot summit, Dr. James Edward Church of the University of Nevada established one of America's first high-altitude meteorological observatories on June 29, 1905. At the observatory, he carried out his famed snow studies and developed the modern science of snow survey. Dr. Church's Nevada system of snow survey is used throughout the world today to predict seasonal water flow from precipitation stored as snow pack. In his honor, the north summit of Mt. Rose has been named "Church Peak.""

When the observatory was originally built, it featured many designs that were unique or revolutionary for its time. The ability to record data without anyone being on site was one of them.

WA 9: Look: EAST: Isn't this a commanding view of Washoe Valley and Washoe Lake?

WA 9: Warning: Sign, "Washoe Valley Wind Alert Turn Radio to 580 AM."

WA 8: Exit 16 – **Note:** To **Alternate/Old US 395**, both south- and northbound. Each route will ultimately loop back to I-580. For a log of

NO EXIT NECESSARY: RENO, NV TO ADELANTO, CA

Alternate/Old US 395 <u>south</u> go to page 108. For a log of Alternate/Old US 395 <u>north</u> go to page 114.

<u>Southbound</u>:

A: Camping: Davis Creek Regional Park is just WEST off the exit. <u>Scan the QR Code in the Index of Websites</u>: **Davis Creek Regional Park** for more information.

A: Bowers Mansion Regional Park offers a playground, seasonal outdoor pool, hiking trails, reservable picnic areas, horseshoe area, and tables/benches. <u>Scan the QR Code in the Index of Websites</u>: **Bowers Mansion Regional Park** for more information.

Bowers Mansion was built in 1863. For a brief but interesting article on the mansion, <u>scan the QR Code in the Index of Websites</u>: **Bowers Mansion history. Bowers Mansion Historic Marker #166** is at the south end of the park. <u>Scan the QR Code in the Index of Websites</u>: **Bowers Mansion Historic Marker #166** to read the text. The Mansion and Park are two miles WEST off the exit. <u>Scan the QR Code in the Index of Websites</u>: **Bowers Mansion** for more information on the mansion and details of tours available.

<u>Northbound</u>:

A: At a little over a mile EAST, the **Chocolate Nugget Candy Factory** is a divine place to stop! The candy makers are "third generation and have been making quality candies and chocolates since 1936."

Outside the store is a short path to a giant miner statue. Owner Ed Feriance says, "He started out in Sparks, Nevada on top of the "Claims Stake Casino" in 1979. That casino only lasted about a year and he was then moved to the Nugget Casino in Reno. We moved him from the Nugget Casino to our Washoe Valley store in 1987. He's 35' tall and made out of fiberglass. Some say he was made from the image of Jack Longstreet the Nevada prospector. He was recently repainted in 2021 and continues to represent the Chocolate Nugget Candy Factory logo. You can visit him in Washoe Valley and get your picture with him." *Scan the QR Code in the Index of Websites*: **Chocolate Nugget Candy Factory** for more information.

A: Camping: About three miles is Eastlake Blvd, the turnoff to **Washoe Lake State Park** on the other side of Washoe Lake. *Scan the QR Code in the Index of Websites*: **Washoe Lake State Park** for more information.

WA 7: Washoe Lake is near Carson City in Washoe Valley. It is a very shallow lake with a surface area that can vary greatly from year to year. The maximum depth is just about 12'. It is made up of two lakes that are connected by a marsh. The lake is eutrophic, meaning it is rich in nutrients to support plant life which in turn depletes the oxygen in the lake killing the fish. Between the shallowness and high winds that can hit the area, the lake is quite turbid. Droughts in past years have caused the lake to dry up entirely, most recently in 1992, 1994, and 2004. On the other hand, in wet years, the lake can lap at the freeway guardrail.

WA 6: Warning: The three-lane freeway transitions to two lanes. Speed limit 70 mph. Wild horses can be seen throughout the valley.

WA 5: Look: WEST: Little evidence remains of the Little Valley Fire, other than the dead toothpick-looking snags lining the hillside. The fire ripped through Washoe Valley at 12:30 AM in the middle of the night of October 14, 2016, burning 2,291 acres and twenty-three homes, one owned by Bunny Ranch owner Dennis Hof. The fire was a direct result of the Nevada Division of Forestry pulling crews off a prescribed burn after a high-wind forecast. The fire escaped when winds were 19 mph with gusts to 87 mph. *Scan the QR Code in the Index of Websites*: **Little Valley Fire** to read an interesting article about Dennis Hof and the fire.

WA 3: Exit 12 – Bellevue Road. EAST will access Washoe Lake. WEST will access Alternate/Old US 395, both south- and northbound.

A: Toiyabe Golf Club is a little over one mile WEST then turn SOUTH on Alternate/Old US 395. The golf club is open to the public. For more information *scan the QR Code in the Index of Websites*: **Toiyabe Golf Club**.

WA 1: Warning: Speed limit 65 mph.

NO EXIT NECESSARY: RENO, NV TO ADELANTO, CA

WA 1: Exit 10 – Eastlake Blvd. EAST, is an eleven-mile loop that will take you to Washoe Lake State Park and ultimately Alternate/Old US 395 North. WEST is to Alternate/Old US 395 North. For a mile-by-mile log northbound go to page 111.

A: Camping: About four miles EAST is **Washoe Lake State Park**. *Scan the QR Code in the Index of Websites:* **Washoe Lake State Park** for more information.

J. BUTLER KYLE

Carson City, Nevada

CC 9: Carson City [Milepost Sign designated as **CC**] is officially the Consolidated Municipality of Carson City, since statehood in 1864. It is an independent city, which means it isn't in a county. Its square miles are 157, a little over Reno's 111 square miles in size. Carson City is also the capital of Nevada (self-guided tours of the capital are available weekdays) and was named after the mountain man Kit Carson. The town began as a stopover for California-bound emigrants on the California Trail. In 1860 it was a regular stop on the Overland Mail Route and the Pony Express. The population is around 58,000. US 395 is only nine miles in distance through Carson City.

In 1995, Carson City became an official Tree City USA. Tree City USA is a program within the Arbor Day Foundation that began in 1976 and is their oldest program. It provides communities with a four-step framework to maintain and grow their tree cover. They believe a thriving urban forest offers many advantages to communities, including cooler temperatures, cleaner air, higher property values, and healthier residents.

The National Arbor Day Foundation's four standards to being named an official Tree City USA are: having a tree board or department in place; a tree-care ordinance; a community forestry program with an annual budget of at least $2 per capita; and hosting an Arbor Day observance and proclamation.

J. BUTLER KYLE

Arbor Day is a day set aside that encourages tree planting and care. It was founded by J. Sterling Morton in Nebraska in 1872 and is celebrated each year on the last Friday in April.

Since 2018, Carson City is also a Bee City USA, the only one in Nevada. The focus of Bee City USA is bees, primarily native species. The steps that affiliates take to conserve native bees include creating safe habitats that are rich in a variety of native plants, providing nest sites, and are protected from pesticides; also hosting community events. Besides bees, other pollinators include butterflies and moths, as well as the non-native honey bee.

The United States is home to just over 3,600 native (wild) bee species. The value of crop pollination has been estimated between $18 and $27 billion annually in the US.

CC 9: Exit 8 – North Carson Street, this is an Exit Only lane. West Side Historic District, Carson Tahoe Regional Medical Center Hospital, and US 395 Business Route. For a log of attractions through Carson City go to Business Route S on page 119. This route reconnects in six miles with US 395 southbound or a return to I-580/US 395 northbound.

Warning: Exit 8 is an 8% downgrade. Speed limit 45 mph.

CC 9: Note: The following is a list of the Exit numbers and correlating streets through Carson City:

Exit 6 – College Parkway.

Exit 5 – US 50. (EAST) Dayton, Fallon, and Virginia City National Historic Landmark. (WEST) Downtown Carson City. This underpass is adorned with a beautiful display of metal Freeway Art depicting the old V&T Railroad roundhouse.

Exit 3 – Fairview Drive.

CC 9: Look: On either side of the freeway is metal art. It was first displayed along the freeway corridor in 2012, but the seed was planted by a volunteer group of gardeners, (GROW - Gardeners Reclaiming Our Waysides), in 1997

NO EXIT NECESSARY: RENO, NV TO ADELANTO, CA

to begin planning the entire I-580 xeriscape landscaping and artwork as part of the federal highway beautification requirement.

It begins with the dramatic eagle and deer you see here as you first descend into the valley. They were designed by Paul Kahn of Winston and Associates and brought to life by Colorado artist Mario Miguel Echevarria.

The overpasses and under the bridges show scenes that highlight the unique history of our community and state. Nevada Division of Transportation Landscape Architect Supervisor John L'Etoil said, "The Transportation Department believes it's important to invest and improve the quality of life of the traveling public as well as the communities our work impacts."

CC 5: Pony Express Trail crossing: There isn't a sign to show where the Pony Express crossed into Carson City, but it is near here. The Pony Express was a wildly fantastic, but short-lived mail route that operated between April 1860 and October 1861. Young men and older boys would mount horses simultaneously and leave Sacrament, California, and/or St. Joseph, Missouri to make the flying trek in as little as ten days across the 1,800 miles of wilderness and hostile territory. Most legs were ten miles where a fresh horse would be waiting for them. With the finishing of the transcontinental telegraph, the Pony Express rode into the history books.

To see an interactive map, <u>scan the QR Code in the Index of Websites</u>: **Pony Express Trail crossing**. On the left side of the screen are the various trail layers. This is where you can unclick as many trails as you want. The Pony Express trail is indicated by the red line.

CC 5: Look: The Fifth Street overpass metal artwork features a cattle drive. This stretch of road is the Carson City Deputy Sheriff Carl Howell Memorial Freeway.

CC 5: Look: WEST: The "C" on the far hills is for Carson High School. It is the only letter on the US 395 corridor accompanied by an American flag.

CC 4: Look: The Fairview Drive overpass metal artwork features early explorer John C. Frémont receiving a welcoming gift of pine nuts from the

Washoe Tribe, the Pony Express, and a pack mule train, as well as steel sculptures.

CC 3: Look: The Koontz Lane overpass metal artwork features Basque sheepherders with their flocks, and the columns represent the aspen trees where the Basque left their carvings.

CC 2: Look: The Clearview Drive overpass metal artwork features a pioneer theme with a wagon train, and metal fish along the edge.

CC 1: Look: A sign indicates this is the end of the Alternative Fuels Corridor for electric vehicles (EV).

Alternative Fuels Corridors, or areas of alternative fuel and began being designated in 2017. An *Alternative Fuels State-of-the-Practice Review Final Report* was published in February 2019. It claimed, "...estimates suggest more than 800,000 alternative fuel vehicles currently operate on US roads, and more than 23,000 public facilities are available for fueling these vehicles." Six alternative fuel vehicle types are being promoted for use on highways by the US Congress: Electric (EV), Compressed Natural Gas (CNG), Liquefied Natural Gas (LNG), Hydrogen, Propane (LPG), and Ethanol (E85). The report includes concerns about adding extra signage to already congested visibility. Although extensive in nature, this report isn't entirely boring. This is a PDF file, to read more *see the website address listed in the Index of Websites*: **Alternative Fuels Corridor.**

CC 1: Look: The sound walls through here feature exquisite basket designs on famed Washoe basket weaver Dat-So-La-Lee. You can see more of those designs by driving along Snyder Avenue.

CC 1: Look: The Snyder Avenue overpass metal artwork features natural scenes reflecting the Washoe Tribe heritage, including the name "uše we? Wat'a", which translates to "Rabbit Drive Creek", the original name for the area.

CC 1: Warning: Speed limit 50 mph. I-580/US 395/US 50 interchange. Left three lanes turn south to continue on US 395.

NO EXIT NECESSARY: RENO, NV TO ADELANTO, CA

CC 1: Note: At the interchange, to reach Lake Tahoe, continue straight on US 50 W. This highway stretches from coast-to-coast, California to Maryland. The highest point before Lake Tahoe is Spooner Summit, 7,146'. Near the summit, both the Pacific Crest Trail and Tahoe Rim Trail can be accessed.

The right lane turns north on South Carson Street and north up US 395 Business Route. For a log of attractions through Carson City go to Business Route N on page 123.

This route reconnects in six miles with I-580/US 395 northbound.

CC 1: Look: NORTH: The metal eagle sculpture landing in the tree weighs in at 800-pounds and has a 16' wingspan. The design was commissioned by the Nevada Department of Transportation and welded by an Idaho artist for around $40,000.

Douglas County, Nevada

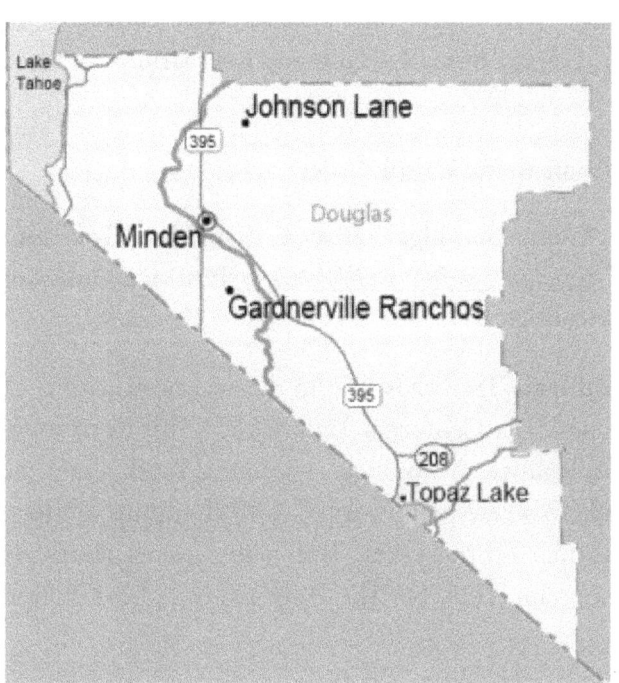

DO 33: Douglas County [Milepost Sign designated as **DO**] has a population of around 49,000. The county seat is Minden. Douglas County holds the first permanent settlement in Nevada, Genoa. The town of Genoa was originally settled in 1851 by Mormon traders selling goods to settlers on their way to California. The county was named after Stephen A. Douglas, famous for his 1860 Presidential campaign and debates with Abraham Lincoln. Douglas County was one of the first nine counties formed in 1861 by the Nevada territorial legislature. At 738 square miles, it is about three-quarters the size of the state of Rhode Island. US 395 travels 33 miles through Douglas County.

DO 33: Warning: Speed limit 55 mph.

DO 33: A: WEST: Turn on Jacks Valley Road for golf courses, hiking, biking, and equine trails, the **Town of Genoa**, as well as the **California Trail Auto**

J. BUTLER KYLE

Tour Route. *Scan the QR Code in the Index of Websites:* **California Trail Auto Tour Route** for a PDF file to read more about the history of this area beginning on page 41.

A: EAST on North Sunridge Drive is **Sunridge Golf and Recreations**. *Scan the QR Code in the Index of Websites:* **Sunridge Golf and Recreations** for more information.

DO 33: What a view! Welcome to the Carson Valley.

DO 32: A: EAST on South Sunridge Drive is **Sunridge Golf and Recreations**. *Scan the QR Code in the Index of Websites:* **Sunridge Golf and Recreations** for more information.

DO 31: Look: EAST: **California Trail crossing:** In the near north corner of the parking lot of the RV park is a California Trail marker. This third route crossed over US 395 in this vicinity. The pioneers continued south along the foothill of the Sierra Nevada to where present-day CA 88 climbs up to Hope Valley and over into California's central valley. This route is more familiarly known as the Mormon-Emigrant Trail, but the Pony Express also followed along this trek.

To see an interactive map, *scan the QR Code in the Index of Websites:* **California Trail Crossing**. On the left side of the screen are the various trail layers. This is where you can unclick as many trails as you want. The California Trail is indicated by the green line. The Pony Express is a red line.

DO 30: Note: Nevada State Historic Marker #123 **"Cradlebaugh Bridge"**, was once located near this bridge.

> "The remains of Cradlebaugh Bridge, built in 1861 by William Cradlebaugh, stand .25 mile westward. That bridge shortened the distance from Carson City to Aurora in the then booming Esmeralda Mining District.
>
> There were two routes from Carson City south to the bridge where they joined, crossed the river and headed into the desert. One

followed the west side of the Carson River; the foothill alternate went via Jacks Valley and the old John James Ranch, then around the hill to the bridge. Five miles south of Cradlebaugh Bridge the road passed Desert Station, a lively hostelry, and beyond, the Twelve Mile House en route to Esmeralda.

The road and bridge were purchased by Douglas County in 1895 for $4,000."

DO 29: A: EAST on Stephanie Way will take you to the trailhead for **Bently Heritage Trail** (about half a mile up the road), Johnson Lane Park (almost three miles), BLM Public Lands access to Johnson Lane OHV via East Valley Road, and Stephanie Way Equestrian Staging Area (about three and a half miles). Johnson Lane Park offers picnicking, restrooms, dog park, playground, baseball diamond, and tennis court. *Scan the QR Code in the Index of Websites*: **Bently Heritage Trail** for more information.

DO 27: A: EAST on Johnson Lane will take you to the BLM Public Lands access to **Johnson Lane Off Highway Vehicle area** where there are miles of beginner, novice-friendly ATV trails as well as challenges for the more experienced. For more information *see the web address in the Index of Websites*: **Johnson Lane OHV.**

DO 27: Look: EAST: That ridgeline is the **Pine Nut Mountains**, a forty-mile north-south range. They take their name from the Pinyon pines that dominate the slopes between 5,000' and 7,000'. The highest mountain is Mount Siegel at 9,456'. Historically, and even today, the Washoe tribe use the Pinyon pine nuts as a staple in their diet.

DO 27: A: EAST to **Minden-Tahoe Airport** on Airport Road/SR 759. The Carson Valley is known for its world-class gliding. The thermals created by the surrounding mountains and prevailing weather patterns create spectacular flight conditions. Many records have been broken here, and pilots come from across the country and around the world to set their own records. Both glider rides and skydiving are available.

DO 26: A: WEST on Genoa Lane/SR 206 to **Genoa**, Nevada's oldest permanent settlement, founded in 1851. Originally named Mormon Station (as its first settlers were Mormons), it started as a trading post and provisioning station to serve passing wagon trains along the Emigrant Trail. Today it is famous for its historic charm, and Candy Dance festival held in September.

A: WEST on the corner of Genoa Lane and US 395 is Nevada Historic marker #12 **"Birthplace of Nevada."**

> "Carson Valley is the Birthplace of Nevada. By 1851, people settled at a place they called Mormon Station, renamed Genoa in 1856. With the early establishment of a post office and local government, the community can lay claim to the title of "Nevada's first town."
>
> Thousands of emigrants moved over the old road skirting the west bank of the Carson River as they prepared to cross the Sierra, feeding their livestock on grass cut along the river. At Genoa; at Mottsville, settled in 1852; and at Sheridan, settled by Moses Job about '54; emigrants stopped to enjoy produce of the region's first gardens. Pony Express riders used this route in 1860, switching a year later to the shorter Daggett Trail, now Kingsbury Grade."
>
> Nevada Centennial Marker No. 12
>
> State Historic Preservation Office

DO 25: Note: WEST on Muller Lane/SR 757 will take you to Kingsbury Grade/SR 207 to Lake Tahoe, US 50, and Heavenly Ski Resort.

DO 25: Warning: Speed limit 55 mph transitioning quickly to 45 mph.

DO 24: Minden is an unincorporated town with a population of about 3,000 at 4720' elevation. It was founded in 1906 by Heinrich Friedrich Dangberg Jr. He named it after the town near his father's birthplace. A large share of the first settlers were German. Dangberg commissioned most of the town's early buildings. Minden has had a Post Office since 1906. It is a unique town among the towns in Nevada, and probably even among towns in the United States.

NO EXIT NECESSARY: RENO, NV TO ADELANTO, CA

It was mapped and defined on the ground before a building was erected. As a result, its neatly laid out streets served as the guide for growth during the first fifty or so years.

A: About a mile into Minden is the Historic Downtown area.

A: EAST: Across the street from the corner of US 395 and Esmeralda Avenue is Nevada Historic Marker #130 **"Minden."**

> "Minden, the seat of Douglas County since 1916, was named for a town in Westphalia, Germany, where the founder of the H.F. Dangberg Land and Live Stock Company was born in 1829. The company established Minden in 1905 to provide terminal facilities for the Virginia and Truckee Railroad, which was then extending a branch line southward from Carson City. The passenger and freight depot was situated at this point.
>
> Principal promoter of the town and it related development was H.F. Dangberg, Jr., secretary of the company and son of the founder."
>
> State Historical Marker No. 130
>
> Nevada State Park System & Carson Valley Historical Society

DO 24: Note: EAST on Ironwood Drive is **Carson Tahoe Minden Medical Center** and **Carson Valley Medical Center**, both have Urgent Care facilities.

DO 24: A: Turn WEST into Ironwood 8 Cinema Plaza to reach **Marsha's Park**, a pretty area with a bench seat and three interpretive placards at the base of the rearing horse and cowboy statue titled "End of the Cattle Drive."

The first plaque is dedicated to Marsha's Park and reads:

> "He plants trees to benefit another generation. – Caecilius Statius, 220-168 B.C.
>
> Like the cowboy in the "End of the Cattle Drive" statue, Marsha Tomerlin exemplifies the spirit of the West. Her vision for this

community has inspired many projects that have benefited the valley over the years, among them this park with its trees.

The year was 1987. Soon after the century-old cottonwoods lining U.S. Highway 395 were felled to make room for widening the main road through the Carson Valley, Marsha and other community citizens took action. Wanting to see trees lining the highway once again, they formed the Beautification Club.

Donations of money, resources, and time made it possible for the new nonprofit club to plant more than 375 trees along the highway from Muller Lane to the Cradlebaugh Bridge. Once again, hawks and other birds of prey had a place to roost. Red-tailed hawks, prairie falcons, turkey vultures, and eagles are just a few of the raptors that perch among "Marsha's trees."

Olive and oak trees, with their seasonal colors, now flourish among the evergreens. Valley residents enjoy tracking the growth of the trees over the years. Twinkling lights bedeck the trees during the holiday season, adding to the festive atmosphere in the community.

The Beautification Club also created a landscaped area, a tiny park, at the intersection of U.S. Highway 395 and State Route 88. The club planted grass and installed sprinklers and lights to create an inviting portal to the Carson Valley. Magnificent evergreens planted in the park extend their boughs in welcome to residents and visitors.

Carson Valley celebrated Marsha's 50th birthday with the installation of a flagpole in the park. The flagpole was a gift from Marsha's associates at her real estate firm.

The Autumn Hills fire in 1996 and the flood in 1997 spurred other community Johnny Appleseeds to action. They created the nonprofit Carson Valley Reforestation and Beautification Foundation to help raise funds for replanting the burned and water-eroded areas and continuing with the beautification of the valley.

In the late 1990s, Marsha Tomerlin agreed to let the new foundation take over the care and planting of trees in the "395 project" that she had started a decade before. The foundation has since planted thousands of seedlings and hundreds of trees, installed a drip system, and installed many raptor perches along U.S. Highway 395 north of Minden.

The Town of Minden voted in 2006 to assume responsibility for maintaining the little park that Marsha had created.

In recognition of Marsha Tomerlin's vision and dedication to creating a beautiful entryway to the Carson Valley, the small park was named "Marsha's Park" in 2006.

Welcome to our beautiful community! Enjoy your stay."

The second plaque is for the horse and rider statue, and reads:

"Dedicated to the men and women of the H.F. Dangberg Land and Livestock Co. Minden, Nevada. 1856-1976." It was "Donated by Larry R. Willson (1952-2003.) Larry spent his childhood on the Dangberg Ranch. Toward the end of his shortened life, he commissioned this statue as a tribute to the role models he looked up to at the ranch. He succumbed to the effects of Lou Gehrig's disease on September 17, 2003."

A myth that surrounds a statue of horse and rider is how many legs the horse has in the air reveals information about how the rider died. On a statue of a horse and rider with both legs in the air means they died during a battle; one leg in the air means they died later of wounds inflicted during a battle. In the case of this statue, the rider didn't go to battle.

The third plaque is in recognition of the "History of the Dangberg Home Ranch," and reads:

J. BUTLER KYLE

"The Home Ranch served as the main headquarters and home for H.F. Dangberg and his family. Dangberg was a tireless worker and a visionary. He was the first to see the great agricultural potential of the Carson Valley and a true pioneer. Dangberg built an empire of ranches and farms. He constructed more dams and dug more ditches and canals in his life than any other man in Nevada. Those canals and reservoirs are still in use today.

Henry F. Dangberg, affectionately known as "Dutch Fred", was born in 1830 in Halle, Westphalia, Germany. He came to the United States in 1848. Dangberg first homesteaded 160 acres in the Carson Valley in 1856 at the site of the Klauber Ranch. "Lucky Bill" Thorington jumped this clam and Fred was forced out. Undeterred, he moved south to the current site of the Dangberg Home Ranch. The original log cabin was constructed in 1857 with timber harvested from the Lake Tahoe basin. It remains as the center portion of the main house.

The massive barn at the Home Ranch was built in the 1870s using wooden pegs as nails. Numerous out-buildings were added through the years. The main house had several additions including the second floor, kitchen, men's dining room and the brick great room.

Dangberg started farming the land around the Home Ranch to provide supplies to the growing population in Virginia City and emigrants on their way to the California Gold Rush. This was the perfect location between the East and West forks of the Carson River. Dangberg understood the value of water rights and he quickly obtained vast plots of land along the Carson River. He dug the first irrigation ditches in the Carson Valley to lead water from the river to his newly cultivated fields. In 1864, he started growing some of the first alfalfa in the state of Nevada. Fred Dangberg married Margaret Gale Ferris in 1865 and they had five children: Fred Jr., John, Eva, George and Clarence.

NO EXIT NECESSARY: RENO, NV TO ADELANTO, CA

Dangberg continued to prosper and acquire more land including the Klauber Ranch in 1902. He wisely shifted the focus of his business from farming to cattle and sheep ranching when the gold and silver boom in Virginia City ended.

H.F. Dangberg died in 1904 and his sons continued to grow the business. The company donated land for the Virginia & Truckee Railroad so that a terminal could be built and the Dangberg founded the town of Minden in 1906. By 1921, they owned a total of 35,597 acres with ranches capable of finishing and marketing 20,000 head of sheep and 2,000 head of beef cattle annually. The Home Ranch was passed to the oldest son, Fred Jr. He and his family lived there until 1988.

The Dangbergs operated two other main ranches in addition to the Home Ranch and Klauber Ranch, namely Sheep Camp and Buckeye Ranch. The Dangberg ranches were totally self-sufficient. They grew all their own vegetables and operated a complete meat processing slaughterhouse. Each ranch had a full-time cook and kitchen. All workers were fed three square meals every day."

To reach Dangberg Home Ranch Historic Park take SR 88 about two and a half miles toward Woodfords and Lake Tahoe.

DO 24: Warning: Trucks use left lane next four miles. The speed limit is 35 mph quickly transitioning to 25 mph through town.

DO 24: Note: Throughout both Minden and Gardnerville are various Electric Vehicle charging stations. *Scan the QR Code in the Index:* **EV Stations - Minden/Gardnerville** for a link to a map of their locations.

DO 23: Note: Driving from Minden into Gardnerville is hard to know where one town ends and the other begins. County Road is in Minden. The next street is Church and that's in Gardnerville.

DO 23: Gardnerville was born of a mix of local economic downturn, marital discord, and thoughts of "what could be" in a dry, 7.5-acre sagebrush-covered flat. Around 1879, Lawrence Gilman bought the land from John and Mary Gardner. The post office was established in June 1881. The town is unincorporated, with a population around 6,000. The community was named after Gardner, a local cattleman. The town became an Official Tree City USA in 2003.

A: During the mining boom of the 1800s, Spanish and French Basques came to the area and learned rather than dig in the hard rock, they were better off providing meat and wool to the miners from their vast sheep herds. **Basque family-style dining** came from their staying in boarding houses with group dining rooms.

For a culinary treat stop at one of the Basque restaurants and try a Picon Punch, the local cocktail of choice.

A: **Carson Valley Museum and Cultural Center** is housed within the historic Douglas County High School building. Designed by the renowned state architect Frederic DeLongchamps—the man responsible for designing most of Nevada's county courthouses and many other buildings throughout the state. The school was built in 1915.

Displays and exhibits share the stories of various past inhabitants of the valley: the American Indian-themed Washo Room features amazing murals with bold colors; the Basque exhibit offers a glimpse into the lonely life of a Basque sheepherder in the surrounding Pine Nut Mountains, with a Basque tree carving (or arborglyph) telling his story; and the Trail to the Promised Land—an exhibit that tells the story of thousands of pioneers who made their way west during the California Gold Rush; and so much more.

DO 23: A: WEST: Located between Gilman St. and Eddy St. is Nevada Historic Marker #129 **"Gardnerville."**

> "Early Gardnerville served the farming community, and teamsters hauling local produce to booming Bodie. The first buildings were a blacksmith shop, a saloon and the Gardnerville Hotel. The latter was moved by Lawrence Gilman in 1879 from the emigrant trail

between Genoa and Walley's Hot Springs where it was known as Kent House, to this site, the homestead of John M. Gardner.

Just as Genoa was the center for British (largely Mormon) settlers after 1851, so Gardnerville, after 1879, became the center for 1870 Danish immigrants. They founded the Valhalla Society in 1885 and met in Valhalla Hall, one block south.

Starting in 1898, Spanish and French Basque shepherds tended some 13,000 sheep in Carson Valley, increasing to 25,000 by 1925, when the Basques began acquiring their own sheep and land. After 1918, several Basques in Gardnerville opened inns which flourished during the Prohibition years."

State Historical Marker No. 129

Nevada State Park System & Cardon Valley Historical Society

DO 22: Look: WEST: Jobs Peak is the highest mountain seen from the Carson Valley. At 10,638', the peak is actually located in California.

DO 19: NA: Entering Washoe Tribe of Nevada and California (Wa She Shu) Indian Reservation. The Washo are a Great Basin tribe of Native Americans. Wa She Shu means, "People from here."

DO 18: A: WEST: Within a few car lengths of each other are Nevada Historic Markers #125 **"Twelve Mile House"** and #131 **"Dresslerville."** Twelve Mile House is WEST in the parking lot just past the Wa She Shu Casino and Travel Plaza. Dresslerville is WEST just off the side of the road a few car lengths past the parking lot.

"Twelve Mile House"

"An important hostelry was so named because of its distance from Genoa and also from Cradlebaugh Bridge across the Carson River. It was built in 1860 by Thomas Wheeler where the Boyd Toll Road to

J. BUTLER KYLE

Genoa and the Cradlebaugh Toll Road to Carson City converged. In this vicinity, a second station was built by James Teasdale.

Twelve Mile House was an important stop on the road to the Esmeralda mining camp of Aurora.

You still see buildings of the original stations here."

State Historical Marker No. 125

Nevada State Park System & Carson Valley Historical Society

"Dresslerville"

"In 1917 State Senator Wm. F. Dressier gave this 40 acre tract to Washo Indians, then living on ranches in Carson Valley. After a school was opened in 1924, it became a nucleus of settlement.

Before the intrusion of Caucasians in 1848, Washos lived in winter in the Pinenut Hills where they stored autumn harvested pinenuts. In summer, they lived in the Lake Tahoe Basin fishing the tributary streams and gathering roots and berries. In fall, they hunted jackrabbits and gathered seeds in Carson Valley.

Their only form of organization was that of kinship.

These stone age people lived in daily communion with giants, monsters, animals whose characteristics were interchangeable with those of people, and with water babies, "having the bodies of old men and the long hair of girls," who lived in the lakes of the High Sierra."

State Historic Marker No. 131

Nevada State Park System & Carson Valley Historic Society

DO 18: Note: Leaving Washoe Tribe of Nevada and California (Wa She Shu) Indian Reservation.

NO EXIT NECESSARY: RENO, NV TO ADELANTO, CA

DO 17: A: Lahontan National Fish Hatchery Complex manages the recovery implementation for the endangered cui-ui *(Chasmistes cujus)* sucker and the threatened Lahontan cutthroat trout (LCT) *(Oncorhynchus clarkii henshawi)*. In historic times, these fish played a key role in the culture and economy of the region.

The cui-ui sucker is found only in the alkaline Pyramid Lake and the lower Truckee River. A "fish lift" helps the suckers around a dam located between the Lake and the River, so they can spawn in the river. The suckers were a major food source for local native American tribes throughout the 1800s.

The largest of the cutthroat family, LCT, were known to reach over forty pounds and regularly migrated one hundred fourteen miles in the Truckee River between Pyramid Lake and Lake Tahoe.

Each year about 300,000 - 400,000 LCT are raised and released by the Hatchery. Currently, the Fish Hatchery produces fish for Pyramid Lake, Walker Lake, the Truckee River, Fallen Leaf Lake, and Marlette Reservoir. Other work includes partnering with Tribal, federal, and state agencies on watershed connectivity, the National Fish Passage Program, river restoration, instream flow development, and fishery monitoring and management.

DO 16: A: WEST: On Washoe Road is a **wildlife viewing area** along the Carson River. There are plenty of places to park and picnic.

DO 16: Warning: Short, one-mile, steep climb.

DO 13: Warning: Four-mile climb with short passing lane.

DO 10: Simee Dimeh Summit, elevation 5,987'. Rather than a pass *over* a hill, this is a 'gap', or rather a low place in a ridge. Originally the name came from the Washoe and means "twin waters" or "double spring", which is the other name the gap is known for.

DO 9: A: WEST: Leviathan Mine OHV access is this route.

DO 9: Look: WEST and EAST: The Tamarack Fire first started July 4, 2021, from a lightning strike in the Mokelumne Wilderness. July 16, 2021, winds blew the fire downslope, and neither ground crews nor air support were able to stop it. The fire spread rapidly causing several communities to evacuate, and many road closures including US 395. At least twenty homes and buildings were destroyed. The fire burned 68,637 acres.

DO 8: A: EAST: Along this stretch of highway is Nevada State Historic Marker #126 **"Double Springs."**

> "Double Springs was the notorious Round Tent Ranch, or Spragues, another station on the road to Esmeralda. Here, James C. Dean, one of the owners and Justice of the Peace in the District in 1864, murdered his wife. This station was connected by the Olds Toll Road with the headquarters of the horse thieves at Fairview.
>
> This was also the place where the Washoe Indian tribe, assisted by their neighbors, the Paiutes, held round dances in the spring to assure the growth of the pine nut, their staple food, and again in the fall for the quality and quantity of the crop.
>
> About four miles north is Mammoth Lodge, post office of the Eagle Mining District, and the polling place in 1861 of the Mammoth precinct of Douglas County. After 1866, it was known as Carter's Station, a stopping place on the road to Esmeralda."
>
> State Historical Marker No. 126
>
> Nevada State Park System & Carson Valley Historical Society

DO 7: Note: The **Walker River Water Shed** drainage basin covers an area of about 3,082 square miles in both Nevada and California. This makes up approximately eighty percent of the total Walker Lake drainage, a lake in Nevada.

DO 6: Look: Straight ahead you can see Antelope Valley, which is in California.

DO 5: A: WEST is a picnic pullout with tables. EAST is a large pullout area.

NO EXIT NECESSARY: RENO, NV TO ADELANTO, CA

DO 4: Holbrook Junction is a community at an elevation of 5,390'. It is at the turnoff of SR 208 to Wellington, Smith Valley, Yerington, and the connector road to Las Vegas.

DO 3: Note: During bad weather in the mountain passes ahead on US 395, SR 208 (towards Yerington) is a good bypass route to reach Bishop, California.

DO 2: Warning: Begin 45-mph speed limit for the next two miles to the California border.

DO 2: Look: WEST: Although much of the black of the burn has healed, the Slinkard Fire began September 6, 2017, with a strike of lightning and burned nearly 9,000 acres.

DO 2: Camping: EAST: **Topaz Lake Recreation Area** has both hookups and primitive camping available. *Scan the QR Code in the Index of Websites:* **Topaz Lake Recreation Area** for more information.

DO 2: Topaz Lake is a reservoir on the California-Nevada border. The modern reservoir was formed by diverting waters from the West Walker River into a nearby basin that had previously contained a smaller, natural lake. The initial dam construction took place in 1922. In 1937, a new levee more than doubled the capacity of the lake. It is three and a half miles long and one and a half miles wide with an average depth of 52' but a maximum depth of 92'.

That original natural lake had historical significance since it lay on the route explorer Jedediah Smith took in late spring of 1827 when he left California at the end of his first journey. This was the first crossing ever of the Sierra Nevada by a non-native. Smith came southeast through Monitor Pass, then east past Topaz Lake into Nevada.

DO 2: A: Topaz Lodge.

"Lunch Break" Review from *Tripadvisor.com*, visited March 2017 by Bob H.

"Passing north along HWY 395, this is a nice stop at a scenic lake overlook. The lake view was actually stunning/brooding at the time, after a late spring snow/rain storm. Salad bar and pulled pork sandwich served us well."

Note: There is a gas station with a nice gift store here, EV Charging Stations, and Casino in the Lodge.

DO 1: A: EAST is a public boat launch for Topaz Lake.

NO EXIT NECESSARY: RENO, NV TO ADELANTO, CA

California Facts and Trivia

Originally the word California referred to the Baja California Peninsula of Mexico. Later it covered what are now the states of California, Nevada, Utah, and parts of Wyoming, Texas, New Mexico, and Arizona. It was in 1845, shortly after President Polk took office, the president had his eye on the area that included San Francisco Bay. Polk wanted it as an American gateway to trade with China and other Asian nations. Following the Mexican American War, California became the 31st state on September 9, 1850.

The state motto is Eureka!, a Greek word translated "I have found it!" It was adopted in 1849 after the discovery of gold in the Sierra Nevada.

California has fifty-eight counties. Alpine County is the least populated with only about 1,000 people. Los Angeles County has the most population with more than 10,000,000 people. More counties in California are named for Saints than any other state.

Most of the food in the US comes from California with over 400 different crops grown. Agriculture is the top industry followed by tourism and technology.

State Nicknames:

The Official state nickname is The Golden State. But before that, after the discovery of gold in 1848, it became known as The El Dorado State. For a time, it was nicknamed The Promised Land, promoting the state as a land of opportunity. Finally, because of the vast number of grapes grown for wine, the state is also known as The Grape State.

California State Symbols:

- Flower: California Poppy
- Bird: California Quail
- Animal: California Grizzly Bear

- Fruit: Avocado
- Vegetable: Artichoke
- Nut: Almond
- Beverage: Wine
- Mineral: Gold
- Gold Rush Ghost Town: Bodie
- Silver Rush Ghost Town: Calico

<u>California Trivia:</u>

- In Pacific Grove there is a law on the books establishing a $500 fine for molesting butterflies.
- The Country Store in Baker has sold more winning California State Lottery tickets than any other outlet in the state.
- If California's economic size were measured by itself to other countries, it would rank the 7th largest economy in the world.
- There are more than 300,000 tons of grapes grown in California annually, and more than 17,000,000 gallons of wine are produced each year. (If you are wondering how much water is used to grow these grapes, an article by NPR's *The Salt* claims anywhere from over two to six gallons of water per one gallon of wine, and that doesn't include irrigation or pre-harvest needs. However, the article goes on to explain how the wine industry has begun changing its methods so as to reduce their water needs, saving millions of gallons per year.)
- It is estimated there are approximately 500,000 detectable seismic tremors in California annually.
- The Iron Door Saloon in Groveland claims to be the oldest drinking establishment in the state. It was constructed in 1852.

Mono County, California

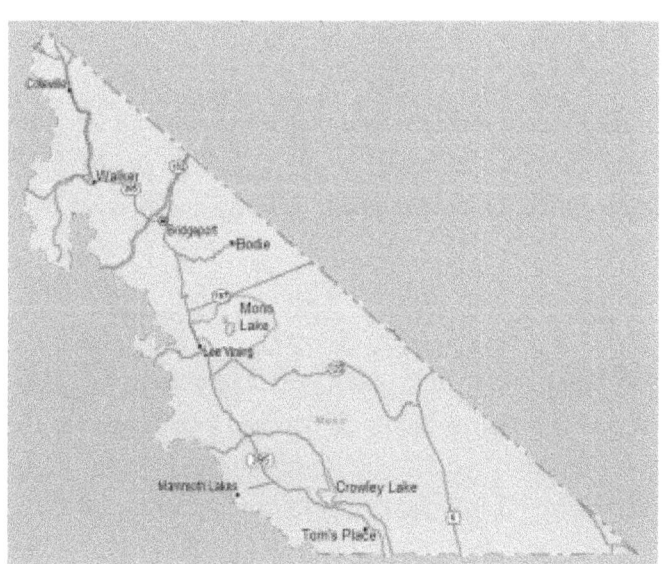

MNO 120: Warning: Begin 55-mph speed limit.

MNO 120: Mono County [Milepost Sign designated as **MNO**] is the fifth-least populated county in the state with less than 15,000 people. At 13,195 square miles, it is about half the size of the state of West Virginia. US 395 travels 120 miles through Mono County.

The county seat is Bridgeport. Mammoth Lakes and June Lake are famous as skiing and fishing resorts with plenty of hiking and biking trails. In the middle of the county is Mono Lake, a vital habitat for millions of migratory and nesting birds. The lake has a wild natural setting, with pinnacles of tufa arising out of the salty and alkaline waters. Also in Mono County is the ghost town of Bodie, just one of more than a dozen.

Little is known about the first inhabitants of the county. But by the time the first English-speaking people came through, a band of Paiute known as the Kuzedika had been there for many generations. These people were hunter-gatherers and the language they spoke was part of the Shoshone language.

The county is named after the Paiute tribe, the Mono people. These people were known as the 'fly people' because fly larvae was their chief food as well as trading stock.

Note: Mono County offers many, many opportunities to see the Autumn colors as the leaves change for the season. *Scan the QR Code in the Index of Websites*: **Mono County autumn colors guide & map** for best viewing locations.

MNO 120: Topaz Agriculture Inspection Station what's the point?

According to a KRNV Channel 4 May 2017 article by Ben Margiott, "California Department of Food and Agriculture believes its stations are the 'first line of defense' against invasive species that, if introduced to crops in the Golden State, could wreak havoc on the massive agriculture industry."

When this story was written, they found that for every dollar spent keeping insects out of California, about $14 was saved in control costs and potential economic losses.

On driving through the Inspection Station, inspectors do a brief visual inspection most of the time before waving the vehicle through, sometimes they ask the traveler if they are carrying any homegrown fruits or vegetables or other inquiries, and occasionally perform physical inspections.

Some of the insects they search for include Japanese beetles, Emerald ash borers, gypsy moths, Mexican fruit flies, and the Asian citrus psyllid, which carries a bacterial disease called Huanglongbing.

The **Sierra Nevada** (Spanish for *snowy range*) lies mostly in central and eastern California. The Carson Range of the Sierra Nevada extends into Nevada and has an average peak height of 10,130'. East to west, the Sierra Nevada varies from 50-80 miles wide. The highest peak is 14,495' Mt. Whitney.

NO EXIT NECESSARY: RENO, NV TO ADELANTO, CA

Running 4,000 miles, the Sierra Nevada is part of the American Cordillera, or chain of mountain ranges, that makes up the "backbone" of North, Central, and South America.

The earliest known inhabitants, discovered from archaeological excavations, were the Martis people of Paleo-Indians. They have been dated in the area from 3,000 BC to 500 AD. Before European exploration and displacement, the Washo and Maidu were in the area.

Various explorers crossed the mountain range between 1827 and the beginning of the gold rush in 1848. Although the first man to use the term Sierra Nevada was Juan Rodríguez Cabrillo in 1542. It wasn't until 1776 Pedro Font, a Franciscan missionary, illustrated a map displaying the name. Fur trapper and mountain man Jedediah Smith and his group crossed the Sierra Nevada at Ebbetts Pass, near Markleville, California on CA 4, in May 1827. In 1833, Joseph Reddeford Walker, mountain man and experienced scout, along with his group started his ascent over the mountains near Genoa, Nevada. Lt. John C. Frémont and Kit Carson were the first Europeans to see Lake Tahoe during the winter of 1844.

At least 300,000 immigrants, merchants, and gold-seekers crossed the Sierra Nevada by 1855. The influx drove the Native Americans out of their homes and food-gathering areas.

Around 1863, the California state legislature authorized Josiah Whitney and a survey crew to officially explore the Sierra Nevada. They began in what would become the backcountry of Yosemite National Park. Mapping and exploring was finished by other people, and by 1912 the United States Geological Survey had published maps of the mountain range.

MNO 119: Antelope Valley runs south for about fifteen miles. The mountains along here rise over 10,000'.

MNO 118: Look: WEST: Turnoff to CA 89 over Monitor Pass, seasonally open, watch for signage.

MNO 117: Topaz (also named Topaz Post Office) is at an elevation of 5,033'. The population is about 50. The Topaz Post Office opened in 1885, but closed in 1922, and then re-opened in 1926. The name was transferred from the original site of the village, which developed on the ranch of T.B. Rickey. Mrs. Rickey named it based on the color of the local quaking aspen trees. The Post Office closed and moved to Coleville in 2018.

MNO 112: Warning: Begin 45-mph speed limit.

MNO 112: Coleville is at an elevation of 5,141' with about a population of 495. It is the birthplace of trick shooter Lillian Smith (1871-1930). It is named after California's first congressman, Cornelius Cole. Cole and his brother went to San Francisco and opened a law firm during the gold rush. Later he entered politics. He died at 102 in Los Angeles, where he lived on a 500-acre ranch in the area that is now Hollywood. The first Post Office at Coleville was established in 1868.

On June 1, 2007, the Larson fire threatened Coleville while burning 1,100 acres and causing $3,000,000 damage.

MNO 110: Meadowcliff Lodge originally opened in November 1959.

MNO 110: California Trail Crossing. This section of the California Trail is known as the Walker River Emigrant Trail. It opened in 1852 and was used for a couple of years. This rugged trail courses slightly southwest through the mountains before turning westbound. Portions of the trail follow CA 108 near Dodge Ridge.

To see an interactive map, *scan the QR Code in the Index of Websites*: **California Trail crossing**. On the left side of the screen are the various trail layers. This is where you can unclick as many trails as you want. The California Trail is indicated by the green line.

MNO 108: A: Look: EAST: Memorial dedicated to Tanker T-130 and crew. The Lockheed C-130 Hercules was flying the nearly 15,000-acre Cannon Fire June 17, 2002. Dedicated June 14, 2003, by the Community of Walker, California, and US Forest Service.

NO EXIT NECESSARY: RENO, NV TO ADELANTO, CA

"In Loving and Grateful Memory of the C-130 Crew" Steve Wass, Craig LaBare, and Mike Davis. "Who gave their lives to save our community on June 17, 2002."

MNO 108: Warning: Begin 45-mph speed limit.

MNO 108: Look: WEST: County Park and **Rest Area** on **Hackney Drive.**

MNO 108: Walker is at an elevation of 5,403', with around a population of 721. Mail to Walker should be addressed Coleville. The town was likely named for pioneer Joseph R. Walker, who started his ascension of the Sierra Nevada range (as part of a longer expedition that ended in Monterey) in nearby Bridgeport.

MNO 107: Look: Ahead: The Mountain View Fire ripped through this community November 17, 2020, burning more than 28,000 acres and destroying nearly ninety homes.

The vicious, southwest-downslope winds gusted from west to east at more than 40 mph for nearly fourteen hours. These winds acted like bellows, very strong and with low humidity. This destructive wind is known as *foehn winds*, the same as the Santa Anas on the west side of the Sierra Nevada. Alex Hoon, a Reno meteorologist with the National Weather Service told the Los Angeles Times, "Winds of this magnitude are uncontainable." A weather front arrived twelve hours too late with rain and snow, aiding the firefighters in all their efforts.

MNO 106: Warning: Begin 55-mph speed limit.

MNO 106: Note: Begin **Eastern Sierra Scenic Byway** which runs North/South and 250 miles south near Coso Junction, California.

MNO 103: Look: EAST: See the large cobblestone remnants shoring up an old road bed?

The **West Walker River** is a tributary of the Walker River. It runs approximately ninety-five miles from eastern California into western Nevada. It drains into Walker Lake Watershed and provides nearly eighty percent of the 3,917 square mile area covered.

The river is eventually diverted through Topaz Lake. The outflow continues on east and is heavily used for irrigation in the valleys.

A record-setting flood in January 1997 destroyed ten miles of the highway. This section of the road was rebuilt in six months. Unfortunately, silt in the raging river settled in Topaz Lake and hurt the trout population.

MNO 101: Note: Elevation 6000'.

MNO 101: Look: WEST: **Shingle Mill Flat** Day Use Park.

The **Humboldt-Toiyabe National Forest** is primarily in Nevada but has small sections in Eastern California. Outside of Alaska, this is the largest US National Forest in the continental US at 6,289,821 acres.

MNO 99: The burned trees you see are from the Boot Fire, which broke out in early September 2018. It charred and burned nearly 7,000 acres. US 395 was closed from Coleville to the Sonora Pass turnoff for nearly two weeks. It took nearly all of those two weeks to contain the fire. The cause of the fire remains still unknown.

MNO 98: Look: WEST: Those avalanche chutes were created by an impressive force of Nature.

MNO 97: A: Camping: To the WEST is **Chris Flat**, a seasonal campground along the West Walker River. *Scan the QR Code in the Index of Websites:* **Christ Flat** for more information.

MNO 94: Warning: Begin 65-mph speed limit.

MNO 94: Look: WEST: Turnoff to CA 108 over Sonora Pass. This road is open seasonally. Watch for signage of open or closed.

MNO 94: Look: EAST: Did you see the phone booth outside the fence of the Sonora CalTrans yard?

The **Sweetwater Mountains** are off to the east. The highest peak is Mount Patterson at 11,654'. The Sweetwaters separate the West Walker River from the East Walker River. Most of the range is only accessible by four-wheel drive vehicles, on foot, or pack animals. And most of the range is contained in the Humboldt-Toiyabe National Forest. The first time the name appears is on the 1874 California Geologic Survey map of California and Nevada.

The type of rock found there is igneous, which is rock formed by the cooling and solidifying of molten material.

MNO 93: Note: Elevation 7000'.

MNO 93: A: Camping: To the WEST is **Obsidian Campground,** a little over three and a half miles in on Forest Service Road 32066. It is a seasonal park in Humboldt-Toiyabe National Forest. Close to both Molybdenite Creek and Little Walker River, the river is stocked with trout. *Scan the QR Code in the Index of Websites:* **Obsidian Campground** for more information.

MNO 92: Look: WEST: **Wheeler Guard Station** in Humboldt-Toiyabe National Forest was first built in 1914. In 1942 conscientious objectors from Civilian Public Service Camp Antelope did considerable renovations on the station. Unfortunately, this made it ineligible for the National Register of Historic Places.

MNO 90: A: Fales Hot Springs. Especially in the winter, steam rises to the west of US 395 from Fales Hot Ditch. It is named after Samuel Fales who purchased the natural hot springs in 1863. Fales turned it into a resort in 1877. The Fales Post Office operated for a short time in 1881. By 1908, Fales Hot Springs was a stagecoach stop and offered baths using the hot water from the springs. Southbound drivers sometimes stop in Bridgeport to report a fire at the junction, thinking the steam rising from Hot Creek is smoke.

According to the records at the Mono County Museum in Bridgeport, Sam Fales transferred control of the facilities to J.M. Mawer in 1908 but lived at the hot springs until he died in 1933 at the age of 104. The resort stayed open under various owners until it exploded in a Butane filling accident in 1952.

Several failed attempts have been made to exploit the minerals around the Hot Spring. The Travertine deposits appear to be too porous to be usable. Uranium was discovered by the Department of Energy but doesn't appear to have been mined. At 413' deep, a test well didn't yield water hotter than 100 °F. The water from the spring is reported to be 180 °F. **Note:** This is private property.

MNO 90: Warning: Uphill grade next two miles.

MNO 88: Devil's Gate Summit, elevation 7,519'. The pass separates the East and West Walker Rivers. It is named for the granite formation, Devil's Gate, to the west.

A: Look: WEST: Monument **"Fremont's Trail 1844."** Plaque Dedicated September 10, 1977. Erected by Bodie Chapter (No. 64) of E Clampus Vitus and Mono County Board of Supervisors

> "On January 27th, a cold, winter day in 1844, Captain John C. Fremont and his guide, Kit Carson, led a small band of half-starved men west past this point. They were in search of the fabled Buena Ventura River, which they believed would give them easy passage through the high range to the west and on to the Fort of John Sutter. A short way northwest of here, they were forced to abandon their Howitzer because of the deep snow, as their tired men could no longer pull the 1500 pound gun and caisson. In desperation, Fremont decided to force a winter crossing of the great Sierra Nevada. They succeeded, and with his band of courageous men reprovisioned themselves at Sutter's Fort and then recrossed the Great Basin, arriving in St. Louis, Missouri on August 6, 1844. A year later, Fremont was back in California and was the United States officer who, on January 13, 1847, received the surrender of the California forces under General Andres Pico at Cahuenga Pass."

MNO 86: Look: EAST: There is a "cell-tree" with a fake but cute little house built under it.

MNO 85: Note: Elevation 7000'.

MNO 76: Bridgeport is the county seat of Mono County. It lies at an elevation of 6,463' in the middle of Bridgeport Valley and was established in 1877. The population is around 575. The first Post Office opened in 1864.

NO EXIT NECESSARY: RENO, NV TO ADELANTO, CA

If you time it right, you can hear the bell tower on the Mono County Courthouse. The courthouse was built in 1880. It is the second-oldest courthouse in the state that has been in continuous operation since it was built.

The ghost story of Sarah, a young woman whose fiancée was killed, haunts Bridgeport Inn's Room 16. The Bridgeport Inn began as a popular stop in 1877 when it was built for Hiram L. Leavitt, a prominent citizen of the town.

A: Mono County Museum.

Note: The Shell station has at least four Electric Vehicle Fast Charging Stations.

MNO 75: A: Bridgeport Reservoir on CA 182, is at the upper end of Bridgeport Valley. Its earth-filled dam was constructed in 1923 by the Walker River Irrigation District, along the East Walker River. The lake primarily provides for agricultural irrigation and flood control for Lyon County in neighboring Nevada.

MNO 75: Look: EAST: **Bridgeport Ranger Station Humboldt-Toiyabe National Forest.** Wilderness permits are available here.

MNO 75: Look: EAST: Did you see the metal horse sculpture in front of the CalTrans yard?

MNO 74: Warning: Begin 65-mph speed limit.

MNO 72: A: Look: The monument, **"Poor Farm"**, is on the WEST side of the highway at Green Creek Road. Turn around and look SOUTH, the location of the poor farm is on the EAST side of the highway at the end of the meadow. Dedicated September 8, 1990. Erected by Bodie Chapter No. 64 E. Clampus Vitus.

> "It began as the county hospital in Bodie in 1879. With the decline of Bodie in mid-1880s the hospital was eventually moved to a site east of this monument and Highway 395 to the rear of the small meadow that you see. At that time it became known as the "Poor Farm", a refuge for the aged, ill and penniless. It continued to operate for several years, but the high cost of maintaining the facility forced

its closure and the buildings and property were put up for bid and sold to a local rancher."

MNO 71: A: Bodie State Historic Park is thirteen miles east on CA 270.

Bodie State Historic Park is a genuine California gold-mining ghost town. You can walk down the deserted streets of a town that once had a population of nearly 10,000 people. The town is named for Waterman S. Body (William Bodey), who had discovered small amounts of gold in the hills north of Mono Lake. In 1875, a mine cave-in revealed pay dirt, which led to the purchase of the mine by the Standard Company in 1877. Miners and other forty-niners flocked to Bodie and transformed it from a town of a few dozen to a boomtown of over 7,000 people.

Designated as a National Historic Site and a State Historic Park in 1962, the remains of Bodie are being preserved in a state of "arrested decay." Only a small part of the town survives. Inside the rooms remain as they were left, even stocked with goods. Today this once-thriving mining camp is visited by tourists, howling winds, and an occasional ghost.

The park closed in December 2016 because of the earthquake in Hawthorne, Nevada, but reopened in 2017.

MNO 71: Warning: Begin 6% seven-mile climb.

MNO 70: Warning: End Daylight Headlight Section.

MNO 70: A: WEST: Monument **"Dog Town 1857."** Plaque placed by the California State Park Commission in cooperation with the Mono County Department of Parks and Recreation and the Mono County Historical Society. September 11, 1966. California Registered Historical Landmark No. 792.

> "Site of the first major gold rush to California's eastern slope of the Sierra Nevada. Dog Town derived its name from a popular miners' term for camps with huts or hovels. Ruins, lying close to the cliff bordering Dog Town Creek are all that remain of the makeshift dwellings which formed part of the 'diggins.'"

NO EXIT NECESSARY: RENO, NV TO ADELANTO, CA

Today, modern day prospectors still look for gold on the slopes of 12,374' Dunderberg Peak, considered the source of the Dog Town placer gold."

A: Monument **"Edge of a Dream."** Erected by Eastern Sierra Scenic Byway.

"Under favorable circumstances it snows at least once every single month of the year in the little town of Mono. Uncertain is the climate in summer that a lady goes out visiting cannot hope to be prepared for all emergencies unless she takes her fan under one arm and her snowshoes under the other." Mark Twain

"Visions of "streets paved with gold" lured many fortune hunters to the Sierra Nevada during the mid to late 1800s. Thousands of gold seekers roamed the hills braving the elements. Life was challenging. Bitter winter winds dropped temperatures well below zero and snowfall was often several feet deep. "Homes" with little or no insulation neither kept the wind out, nor the warmth in. Shortages of provisions, difficult travel conditions, illness, and isolation were some of the many challenges faced by these hardy prospectors and pioneers. Most of the men and women were financially unsuccessful—a lucky few actually realized their dreams."

A: Monument **"Boom and Bust"** Erected by Eastern Sierra Scenic Byway.

"Here today, gone tomorrow" describes many early mining towns—Dog Town was no exception. Miners rushed to the eastern Sierra when gold was discovered in the waters of Dog Creek in the 1850s. The largest nugget ever found on the eastern slope was said to have come from here. Despite the hopeful start, these gold deposits were not very extensive and within a couple of years "placer excitement" shifted to Monoville, a new strike just a few miles south of here."

"Many hopeful parties have tried to make a go of the remaining placer deposits. In the late 1860s and early 1870s, Chinese families occupied stone huts, planted gardens, and lived off what little gold they could find. As late as the early 1900s, an unproductive dredging operation was in place."

"Though never very profitable, Dogtown was significant as the first placer settlement on the eastern slope of the Sierra, bringing attention to many profitable areas such as Bodie, Aurora, Masonic, and Virginia City. In some areas, mining continues today, adding to the wealth of gold and silver already found in these lonely hills."

MNO 68: A: EAST: Monument **"Little Bodie."** Dedicated September 13, 2014. Erected by Ancient & Honorable Order of E Clampus Vitus. 50th Anniversary Bodie Chapter No. 64.

"East of this site was located the Little Bodie Mines. Organized in the 1930s, it was composed of 5 mines or claims, which produced a fine grade ore containing galena, pyrites, sulphides and gold valued at $12 to $15 per ton.

During its heyday, the mines employed 5 workers and could produce 30 tons of ore per day. The facilities included a shop, pump, bunkhouse, mill and settling tank. Water for the milling process was pumped from springs located 300 feet south of the mines. The mineshafts were reportedly 175 feet below the surface and between 100 to 200 feet in length.

By the 1940s, the mines began to falter and soon thereafter all commercial operations ceased. Most of the equipment, machinery and buildings were dismantled and sold.

Although its existence was brief, Little Bodie continued the tradition of being a gold producer started by its namesake "Big Bad Bodie" in the 1860s."

MNO 63: Warning: Begin 6% four-mile downgrade and four-lane highway.

NO EXIT NECESSARY: RENO, NV TO ADELANTO, CA

MNO 63: A: Camping: Turn WEST on Virginia Lakes Road. Six miles in are several lakes for fishing and hiking. Seasonal primitive campsites and resort cabins are also available.

MNO 63: Conway Summit elevation 8,138'. This is the highest point on US 395. Conway Summit is named after John Andrew Conway, a settler in the area in 1880. Geographically, it was formed from an upland plateau by the sinking of the land in the Mono basin area. The Sawtooth Ridge of the eastern Sierra Nevada, topped by 12,279' Matterhorn Peak, rises to the west of the pass. The Bodie Hills lie to the east.

MNO 63: Look: SOUTH: Mono Lake Vista Point has a great view of Mono Lake and several interpretive signs to peruse.

A: Monument **"Mono Diggin's."** Plaque dedicated September 9, 1978. Erected by Bodie Chapter (No. 64) of E. Clampus Vitus.

> "About 1 mile N.E. of here lies Mono Diggins, the first extensive placer mining excitement east of the Sierra. Cord Norst is generally credited with being the discoverer on July 4, 1859. A town, Monoville, boasted a transient population of 500-1,000. A Post Office established December 12, 1859, was closed by April 2, 1862, as the prospectors moved on to Aurora.
>
> One of the most ambitious hydraulic water projects of the time was the transportation of water from Virginia Creek to the diggings by open ditches known as "The Mono Ditch." The remnants of the system may be seen by looking easterly from the highway summit or northerly from the bottom of the grade."

MNO 60: Warning: From the bottom of the summit to Lee Vining heavy crosswinds are normal. Heed windsock warning and flashing signs. Elevation 7,000'. End four-lane highway.

MNO 59: A: WEST: Monument **"Avalanche 1911."** Turn on Mill Creek Powerhouse Road.

J. BUTLER KYLE

Dedicated September 10, 2011. Erected by Bodie Chapter No. 64. E Clampus Vitus.

> "Not far from this site, in the early morning hours of March 7, 1911, a massive avalanche roared down the east slope of Copper Mountain and wiped out the town of Jordan. Eight people were killed including Robert Mason, the chief engineer of the power plant. Only his wife and dog survived.
>
> This snow slide was the worst of several occurring, in and around, Mono County during the winter of 1910-11. Rescuers coming from Bodie and Lee Vining were forced to travel by snowshoes or skis as all roads were impassable.
>
> Additionally, contact with other communities was severed as all telephone lines were down. It took several days to locate and identify all the victims. Most were later buried in a nearby cemetery.
>
> This event was also the death knell for a town slowly recovering from a financial disaster (closure of the local mines, businesses and post office in 1903). Today, remnants of foundations, miscellaneous debris and 8 headstones stand as silent reminders of one of the most devastating events in Mono County history."

The Mill Creek Power Plant was built in 1911 to supply hydroelectricity to the mining towns in the area.

Entering **Mono Basin National Forest**. This is a Scenic Area and was the first one in the United States in 1984. The Inyo National Forest is who administers the Scenic Area. Mark Twain, in his book *Roughing It,* mentioned Mono Lake and the surrounding scenery. <u>Scan the QR Code in the Index of Websites</u>: **Mark Twain** to read the two chapters Twain devoted to Mono Lake.

Mono Lake is also part of the Mono Lake Tufa State Natural Reserve which was created in 1981 to preserve one of the rarest places in the world. Few places have such spectacular "tufa towers," wetlands, and bird habitats.

NO EXIT NECESSARY: RENO, NV TO ADELANTO, CA

Tufa is limestone that forms when underwater springs full of calcium mix with the carbonates in the lake waters. When the water level falls the other-worldly towers are exposed.

MNO 58: Note: Turn EAST on CA 167 to Hawthorne. Several miles down the road is a monument for the Bodie and Benton railroad.

MNO 56: Warning: Begin 60-mph speed limit and two-lane highway.

MNO 56: A: Turn EAST for the Mono Lake Cemetery and Mono Lake Park Nature Trail. The trail is .5 miles long on a nice boardwalk. **Warning:** If you walk out to the tufa towers the mud is as slick as ice!

MNO 56: A: Look: EAST: Monument (hidden behind the cottonwood tree) **"Grave of Adeline Carson Stilts."** Dedicated September 8, 1973. Erected by Bodie Chapter (No. 64) E Clampus Vitus and Mono County Board of Supervisors.

> "In sight of this location is the grave of Adeline Carson Stilts, daughter of scout, guide and explorer Kit Carson. Called "Prairie Flower" by her father, and considered to be his favorite child, she came to the gold site of "Mono Diggins'" with her husband in about 1858. She died in the winter of 1859, at the age of 21, at the home of her friends, known as the Wilson Ranch."

MNO 54: Warning: Begin 50-mph speed limit.

MNO 54: The Marina Fire broke out in 2016. About 650 acres burned along the highway and up the hillside. Over 500 personnel fought the blaze as well as five helicopters. The cause of the fire is unknown.

MNO 53: A: EAST: **Mono Lake Boardwalk** and **picnic access**. The Boardwalk is an easy 0.7-mile walk to the "tufa towers." **Warning:** If you walk out to the tufa towers the mud is as slick as ice!

MNO 52: Warning: Begin 30-mph speed limit.

MNO 52: A: EAST: Mono Basin Interpretive Center opened in 1992 and is excellent. With interactive displays and onsite films, it is well worth taking the time to see.

Mono Lake is thirteen miles long and nine miles wide. It is considered shallow because the average depth is only 57', with a max depth of 159'. The endorheic lake (which means it has no outflow) formed at least 760,000 years ago. The lack of an outlet causes high levels of salts to accumulate in the lake which makes the lake water very alkaline. Scientists believe the lake formed during the Long Valley volcanic eruption.

The ecosystem of the desert lake is unusually productive. A prolific, single-celled planktonic algae is the basis for the whole food chain. Trillions of brine shrimp (*Artemia monica*) found nowhere else on earth, feed on the algae. These tiny shrimps thrive in the alkaline waters and provides critical food for the millions of annual migratory birds that feed on the shrimp and alkali flies. These flies, *Ephydra hians*, walk underwater encased in a tiny air bubble where they graze and lay eggs. Once hatched, they live on shore and feed the migrating and nesting birds. Mono Lake has the second-largest nesting population of California gulls.

High Sierra Brine Shrimp Inc., a Lee Vining-based company, harvest the tiny creatures and sell them to pet stores for exotic fish food or as feed for shrimp farms worldwide.

Mono Lake has been featured in artwork on the cover photo for Pink Floyd's album *Wish You Were Here* (1975) and the Clint Eastwood film *High Plains Drifter* (1972).

In 1930, Los Angeles voters passed a $38.8 million bond to buy land in the Mono Basin and fund the Mono Basin Extension. The 105-mile extension diverted water from the lake causing levels to fall below half its original volume and doubling its salinity. It wasn't until 1994 before concerns were addressed and a water management level was set to a minimum of 6392' above sea level, from a low of 6372' in 1982.

NO EXIT NECESSARY: RENO, NV TO ADELANTO, CA

MNO 52: Lee Vining (formerly Leevining, Poverty Flat, and Lakeview), elevation 6,781'.

The town was named after Leroy Vining, who founded it in 1852 as a mining camp. Unfortunately, he accidentally shot himself in the nearby (ghost) town of Aurora, Nevada. Chris Mattly laid out the town and named it "Lakeview" in 1926. In 1928, after the town tried to get a post office, they learned another town in California already had the name. It wasn't until 1953 the name Lee Vining was chosen. For a while, it was named Poverty Flat for its unfavorable agricultural conditions. Today the economy relies mainly on tourism.

A: Turn EAST on First Street: This is the site of the **Upside-Down House**, a distinctive local landmark, built by silent-film actress Nellie Bly O'Bryan. Here also is the **Mono Basin Museum,** or Old School House Museum, and Guy Hess Community Park which has a picnic area, BBQ stands, and a Tesla charging station.

A: WEST: Halfway through town is monument **"Lee Vining."** Plaque dedicated September 8, 1979. Erected by Bodie Chapter (No. 64) of E Clampus Vitus.

> "The name of this community honors Leroy Vining. In 1852 Lt. Tredwell Moore and soldiers of the 2nd Infantry pursued Indians of Chief Tenaya's tribe from Yosemite across the Sierra via Bloody Canyon. They took back mineral samples and a prospecting party was organized. In this group were the Vinings, Lee & Dick, who established a camp at what is now Lee Vining Creek."

MNO 51: A: Turn WEST on CA 120 to Tioga Pass, a seasonal road. The entrance to Yosemite National Park is eleven miles ahead. A fee is required. Reservations are required at times, <u>scan the QR Code in the Index of Websites</u>: **Yosemite Reservations** for more information.

A: Turn WEST then SOUTH on Vista Point Drive for an **overlook of Mono Lake** and a monument with three plaques. There is a large vehicle turnaround here. Dedicated September 13, 2013. These plaques feature little-known and forgotten facts about Mono Lake. Erected by E Clampus Vitus Bodie Chapter No. 64.

"Mono Lake – Lake of Many Uses"

"Except for fishing, this "Inland Sea" has been a lake of many uses over the years. (Commercial, industrial, recreational, military, medicinal, etc.) Starting in the 1800s and by the 1910s, in and around this body of water, oil drilling and mineral extraction activities took place. By the 1920s it became the venue for: bathing beauty pageants, boat races, swimming competitions and water skiing contests. During the 1930s, a boat tour of the lake and islands was offered, advertised as a visit to the "Tahiti of the Sierras" due to the existence of hot springs on the islands. A Tahitian spa was planned, but never built. In the late 1950s, a public boat dock and marina was built along the west shoreline and operated for several years. And, during the cold war a secret military test site was located along the south shoreline. Although, today, only remnants can be seen of those activities, they made a lasting contribution to the development of Mono County and the Eastern Sierras."

"Mono Lake…?"

"First appearing on official maps in 1854, it is the predominant geological feature of this region and source of many myths, legends and controversies. One unresolved issue – who was the first to document this unique body of water? Was it Jedediah Smith during his trek through the region in 1827? Or was it Joseph Walker in 1833? Perhaps, it was Lt. Treadwell Moore in 1852? Coincidentally, each reported finding a lake with similar features. Another debate is the origin of its name. Some sources report it was named for the Monache Indians, early inhabitants of the area. Other accounts note "Mono" was a Spanish word and cite the majority of California county names were of Spanish origin. Others refer to the Greek word "Monos" meaning – solitary or deserted. Each is a plausible

NO EXIT NECESSARY: RENO, NV TO ADELANTO, CA

explanation. In the late 1800s, this intimidating lake gained international notoriety through the writings of Mark Twain's newspapers articles and his book "Roughing It." What is not in question – Mono Lake was the namesake of the 47th county created by act of California state legislature (SB-199) in 1861."

"Mono Lake & Hollywood"

"This body of water has been the backdrop of many Hollywood and television productions. Two of the first movies filmed here were "Kilowatt, The Conqueror" (1921) and "The Huntress" (1923) staring Colleen Moore. "White Magic" (1930) was one of the first "Talkies" to feature Mono Lake. "The Bride Wore Red" (1937) staring Joan Crawford; "Kim" (1950) staring Errol Flynn; "Fair Wind to Java" (1953) staring Fred MacMurray; and "Jonathan Livingston Seagull" (1973) had second unit photography (background scenes) taken here. Numerous nature films, produced and directed by major studios and independence filmmakers, have told various stories of Mono Lake – its ecology, geography, chronology, etc. Also, many "commercials" and music videos have been filmed here, however, the most recognized and successful movie shot on location here was "High Plains Drifter" (1973) staring Clint Eastwood and served as the stark setting of the fictional western town of Lago. Today, remnants of the volcano set built for the 1953 film can still be seen above the waves on this island sea. As long as Hollywood has need of breathtaking vistas and clear blue skies, Mono Lake will have a continuing role in the film and video industry."

MNO 50: Warning: Begin 65-mph speed limit.

MNO 50: Look: EAST: The slide mountain and crater you see are part of the **Mono-Inyo Craters** which are a chain of volcanic craters, domes, and lava flows that stretch twenty-five miles from Mono Lake to Mammoth Mountain.

The Mono Lake Volcanic field at the most northern edge begins with the two islands in Mono Lake and a cinder cone volcano on its northwest shore. The most recent eruption was about 300 years ago.

MNO 47: A: Turn WEST for **June Lake** scenic loop. This scenic sixteen-mile loop on SR158 takes you past at least four lakes. Recreation, such as hiking or skiing, and camping as well as resort opportunities abound.

MNO 46: A: To the EAST on CA120 is the road to **Mono Lake South Tufa Self-Guided Nature Trail**. Five miles in is parking, there is a per-person parking fee. The South Tufa Self-Guided Tour is a one-mile loop. *Scan the QR Code in the Index of Websites*: **Mono Lake South Tufa Self-Guided Nature Trail** for more information and to listen to the nine-stop narrated tour.

MNO 45: Warning: Begin 5% six-mile climb. **Note:** Elevation 7000'.

MNO 44: Inyo National Forest covers parts of the eastern Sierra Nevada of California and the White Mountains of California and Nevada. Mount Whitney being the highest point in the Contiguous United States is one of several superlatives (meaning an extreme in geography such as highest, lowest, longest, etc.); others found in the Inyo include Boundary Peak, the highest point in Nevada; and the Ancient Bristlecone Pine Forest that protects the oldest trees in the world.

MNO 40: A: June Lake scenic loop on CA158 to the WEST. This scenic sixteen-mile loop on SR158 takes you past at least four lakes. Recreation, such as hiking or skiing, and camping as well as resort opportunities abound.

MNO 38: Look: WEST: Despite looking like a cinder cone, which is defined as a steep conical hill, Wilson Butte is actually a small obsidian/rhyolite dome.

MNO 37: A: Obsidian Dome Road will take you a little over a mile to the base of Obsidian Dome, a mountain made of volcanic glass, or obsidian boulders. The dome formed about 600 years ago. There is a trail around the base of the dome.

NO EXIT NECESSARY: RENO, NV TO ADELANTO, CA

Further on, after the road turns to gravel is **Hartley Springs Campground,** a primitive Forest Service campground. *Scan the QR Code in the Index of Websites:* **Hartley Springs** for more information.

MNO 37: Warning: Avalanche area.

MNO 36: Deadman Summit 8047' elevation, is not marked. **Warning:** Begin 6% two-mile downgrade.

MNO 34: A: Look: WEST: Hidden behind a tree at the bottom of the grade is monument **"Legend of Deadman."** Dedicated September 11, 2004. Erected by Bodie Chapter No. 64 E Clampus Vitus.

> "In 1861 the burned and headless body of Robert Hume, a prospector, was found in a shallow grave not far from this site. Later, the head was located in a nearby stream (now known as Deadman Creek). Hume was last seen alive with his partner, Farnsworth, searching for the fabled Lost Cement Mine. When next seen, Farnsworth was asked about his partner, to which he told a story of a surprise Indian attack and barely escaping with his life. A subsequent investigation proved this to be untrue. Unfortunately, before an arrest warrant could be issued, Farnsworth disappeared.
>
> However, the Legend did not end there. A few years later, the remains of two nameless prospectors were found near the bottom of what is now Deadmans Pass. Then, in December 1879, William Haines a Postal worker, was reported missing during a severe winter storm while transporting mail between Mammoth City and Kings Ranch. His body and mailbags were later recovered near the bottom of what is now – Deadman Summit. Thus, ensuring this section of Mono County would forever be linked with "Deadman.""

MNO 33: A: Crestview Rest Area (previously Crest View) is at an elevation of 7,520'. A resort named Crestview Lodge was built near this area in 1927 by Clarence Wilson. The Rest Area is on the WEST side of the highway. Sometimes it is closed in the winter.

J. BUTLER KYLE

There is a monument a little ways behind the restrooms. **"Lost Cement Mine"** Plaque dedicated September 6, 1980. Erected by Bodie Chapter (no. 64) of E Clampus Vitus.

> "Somewhere near this spot is located the famous Lost Cement Mine. First discovered in 1857, the find was described as a ledge, "wide as a curb stone" of rusty, reddish cement, two thirds of it pure gold. Various circumstances prevented the original discoverers from returning to claim their wealth. History indicates the location of the Lost Cement Mine may have been rediscovered and mined periodically until 1877 and then again concealed. An occasional prospector still searches for the elusive treasure but its location today still remains a secret. If while hiking in the area, you happen to come upon a ledge of pure gold please notify the nearest ECV Chapter so that we might relocate this monument to the correct site."

MNO 31: A: Mammoth Lakes Scenic Loop to the WEST is a sixteen-mile loop that includes the three Inyo Craters, one as deep as 200'. Earthquake Fault, although called a fault, this fissure is more accurately defined as a fracture. The trail to it is .3 miles long. Mammoth Lake offers off-season bike lifts and rentals, plus the Panorama Gondola.

MNO 26: A: Mammoth Lakes scenic loop WEST. Devils Post Pile National Monument can be accessed from this route. Devils Post Pile is a fascinating geologic formation made of a mass of four to seven-sided columns of basalt. Rainbow Falls is a 101' waterfall so named after the shimmering rainbow the mist creates. A shuttle is available, for a fee.

A: The Geothermal plant, interpretive signs and a map of Mammoth Lakes, and a monument are under the bridge and to the EAST side of the highway. **"Casa Diablo."** Dedicated September 8, 2001. Erected by Bodie Chapter #64 E Clampus Vitus.

> "A distinctive landmark and gathering place used by many early inhabitants of the area for bathing, food preparation, ceremonial and medicinal purposes. It was named "House of the Devil", by early

explorers, for its boiling hot springs, plumes of rising steam and spectacular geysers.

From 1878 to 1881 it was a stage stop along the Bishop Creed-Bodie Stage Route, a vital relay station for supplies, mail and equipment en route to the mining camps of Mammoth City, Mill City, Mineral Park and Pine City. Unfortunately, when those mines failed, Casa Diablo faltered.

After its tenure as a stage stop, Casa Diablo endured a succession of business ventures (trading post, seasonal resort, tavern, gas station, grocery store, hardware store and lumber yard) until 1983, when it was transformed into a geothermal electric generating plant.

Although today remnants are all that remain of Casa Diablo, it made a lasting contribution to the development of Mono County and the Eastern Sierra."

MNO 23: Mammoth Yosemite Airport (FAA Identifier: MMH) is a town-owned public airport. It is also known as Mammoth Lakes Airport or Mammoth-June Lake Airport. Although mainly used for general aviation, there are seasonal scheduled passenger flights into and out of the airport also.

MNO 22: A: Turn WEST on Convict Lake Road. Two miles along the road is Convict Lake. A three-mile-long trail encircles the lake. The lake was named in the fall of 1871 when convicts escaped from Carson City, Nevada, and were trapped by the posse. After a shootout left two locals dead, the prisoners were caught and dispatched with frontier justice.

MNO 21: Look: EAST: Isn't that the prettiest little church?

John Muir Wilderness is a wilderness area that runs along the crest of the Sierra Nevada for ninety miles from near Mammoth Lakes at the north end to Cottonwood Pass near Mount Whitney in the south. Created in 1964 by the Wilderness Act and named for naturalist John Muir, it is 581,000 acres. The John Muir Wilderness contains the largest contiguous area above 10,000' in the continental United States.

MNO 19: Crowley Lake was created in 1941 when the Los Angeles Department of Water and Power built a dam on the Owens River. The reservoir acts as flood control and is used for storage for the Los Angeles Aqueduct.

The lake is named after Father John J. Crowley. Known as "the desert Padre", Crowley had a significant impact on Owens Valley history. When agriculture became impossible after Los Angeles began siphoning off water from the valley, Crowley encouraged the residents that the Valley could become a tourist destination.

Today, Crowley Lake is known for its trout fishing- cutthroat, brown, and rainbow. Every year upwards of 10,000 anglers arrive for opening day. The largest brown trout ever caught weighed a whopping twenty-six pounds!

Crowley Lake is in Long Valley Caldera, one of the world's largest calderas at twenty miles long, eleven miles wide, and up to 3,000' deep.

A: Crowley Lake Columns were an oddity on the eastern shores from the time the reservoir was completed. As high as 20', some people described them as "stone cylinders connected by stone arches." In 2015, geologists discovered the columns formed when the frigid snowmelt seeped down through the volcanic ash creating tiny holes. This resulted in boiling water and steam that came back up through the holes. There are nearly 5,000 of these pillars.

A 4.2-mile, moderately-difficult trail can be trekked to reach the columns. <u>Scan the QR Code in the Index of Websites</u>: **Crowley Lake Columns** for more information including a map.

MNO 18: A: Turn WEST to reach the **"McGee Mountain Rope Tow" #34** monument on Crowley Lake Drive. Dedicated September 14, 1996. Erected by Bodie Chapter No. 64 E Clampus Vitus.

> "The first permanent rope tow in the Eastern Sierra was built west of this site on the east slope of McGee Mountain. This predecessor of Mammoth Mountain Ski Area was constructed here in 1938 because of its dependable snow and nearness to a highway. Prior to this facility most down hill skiing was done by use of a portable

rope tow system (a working gasoline engine, rope, and pullies.) Dave McCoy- world class skier, entrepreneur, and visionary, was instrumental in organizing and promoting skiing here. The success of this rope tow motivated McCoy to move in 1941 to Mammoth Mountain. Subsequently, within a few years, the popularity of skiing here declined and this rope tow was abandoned. Some remnants of that first rope tow can still be seen today along the slopes of McGee Mountain."

Note: US 395 can be reached by continuing south on this road.

A: Camping: Off Crowley Lake Road is **Crowley Lake BLM Campground**. There are tent and RV sites. *Scan the QR Code in the Index of Websites*: **Crowley Lake Campground** for more information.

A: At Hilton Creek is a monument dedicated to **John J. Crowley** by the Department of Water and Power City of Los Angeles 1941.

"Crowley Lake

Dedicated to the memory of the Padre of the Desert. The very Reverend Monsignor John J. Crowley. December 8, 1891 – March 17, 1940

In recognition of his high citizenship and unselfish service to the people of Inyo – Mono."

MNO 15: A: This vista point has three interpretive signs WEST off the highway. **"A Big Blast in the Past: The Long Valley Caldera"**, **"Crowley Lake: Water for Los Angeles, Enjoyment for Anglers"**, and **"Mountains and Moraines."** "Mountains and Moraines" is a panorama of the mountain elevations. These signs are presented by Eastern Sierra Scenic Byway.

MNO 13: Look: WEST: Oft times, across the crooked creek, there is a herd of sheep and a Basque camp near that old cabin.

MNO 11: Look: EAST *really fast*: There's a really cool round house on rocks against the hill.

MNO 11: Tom's Place (formerly Hans Lof's) is at an elevation of 7,090'. In 1919, Hans Lof started a resort by that same name. A couple of years later, Tom Yernby bought the place in 1922 and renamed it. The Tom's Place Post Office opened in 1963. James Whitmore, long time actor whose career spanned from 1949 to 2005, owned several homes and made it his primary residence for many years. Members of his family may still live there.

MNO 11: A: Camping: Tuff Campground is a Forest Service campground. Scan the QR Code in the Index of Websites: **Tuff Campground** for more information.

A: This is the southern end of **Crowley Lake Drive.**

MNO 8: Sherwin Summit 7000'. **Warning:** There is a pull off for brake check area. Begin 6% downgrade for eight miles. Valley floor elevation 4425'.

Off to the EAST are the **White Mountains** of California and Nevada. They range across the upper Owens Valley for approximately sixty miles. Triangular in shape, they are about twenty miles wide at the southern end, and narrow to a point at the north. The elevation generally increases south to north.

Cattle graze by permit up to the alpine zone. There were many Bighorn Sheep in the mountains until domestic sheep were introduced and brought disease that decimated the Bighorn population. The population is slowly recovering. Paiute Indians had summer hunting camps near 13,100', leaving ruins of archeological interest.

White Mountain Peak (or simply White Mountain), at 14,252' is east of Tom's Place. It is the highest peak in the White Mountains, the highest peak in Mono County, and the third-highest peak in the state after Mount Whitney and Mount Williamson. It is the 14th-most topographically prominent peak in the contiguous United States.

NO EXIT NECESSARY: RENO, NV TO ADELANTO, CA

MNO 5: A: Look: WEST: Vista point and interpretive signs. **"Range of Light: Sculpted by Ice", "Wilderness: An Enduring Resource",** and **"Life on the Edge."** These signs are presented by Eastern Sierra Scenic Byway.

MNO 4: Leaving Inyo National Forest. The National Forest has been the scene for several movies. *Ride the High Country,* 1962, starred Randolph Scott and Joel McCrea. Steve McQueen was in the 1966 *Nevada Smith.* Charlton Heston was in *Will Penny* in 1968. The movies *Joe Kidd* 1972 and *High Plains Drifter* 1973 both starred Clint Eastwood. *Star Trek Insurrection,* the 1998 Sci-fi film, and BBC's *Walking with Monsters,* the second half of the second episode set in Early Permian Germany, were both filmed in the National Forest.

MNO 1: Note: Elevation 5000'.

Inyo County, California

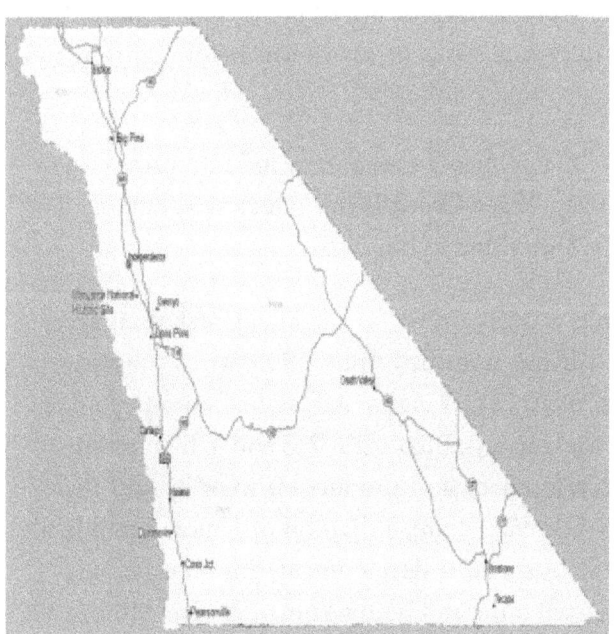

INY 130: Inyo County [Milepost Sign designated as **INY**] is in the Heart of El Camino Sierra. Independence is the county seat. The county may have mistakenly been named after the chief, or headman, of the Panamint band of Paiute-Shoshone people. This area was the historic homeland of the Owen Valley Paiute, Mono tribe, Coso people, Timbisha, and Kawaiisu Native Americans.

Inyo County boasts many superlatives from Mount Whitney the highest point in the contiguous United States to Badwater Basin in Death Valley the lowest point in North America. From Methuselah, an ancient Bristlecone pine tree and one of the oldest living trees anywhere, to Owens Valley, the deepest valley on the American continents. It has two mountain ranges that are higher than 14,000' – the Sierra Nevada and the White Mountains. Thirteen of California's fifteen peaks are higher than 14,000'. There are at least fifty ghost towns.

The County's population is around 19,000, a little under half the size of the state of Virginia. US 395 travels 130 miles through Inyo County.

INY 129: The Round Fire near Rovana, WEST, swept through this area on February 7, 2015, at 20:30. More than three dozen homes and buildings were destroyed. The fire forced the evacuations of two towns before burning more than 7,000 acres.

INY 129: A: At the base of the grade is a monument and interpretive signs to the WEST side of the highway. **"Pine Creek Mine"** Dedicated June 27, 1987. Erected by E Clampus Vitus Slim Princess No. 395.

> "West of this spot, gold was discovered in the Pine Creek drainage by Civil War Veterans. It was not until April, 1916, when tungsten was discovered by four men: O.E. Vaughn, A.E. & C.C. Beauregard, and James Sproul, on their claims, Blizzard 1, 2, 3 and 4, high on the mountain. Years of development and production went by and the mine was acquired by U.S. Vanadium, a division of Union Carbide Corp., on May 14, 1936. After more development, this mine became the world's largest tungsten mine and is now known as "The Mine in the Sky.""

INY 128: Look: WEST: Did you see the rock wall and foundation alongside the road? These rock fences may go back to an era of pioneer settlement in Round Valley. With few trees in the valley, fences were constructed with rocks to hold in their cattle and horses.

INY 121: A: Camping: Six miles northwest is **Millpond Campground**. _Scan the QR Code in the Index of Websites_: **Millpond Campground** for more information.

INY 119: A: EAST is a monument of the **"Lynching of the Convicts."** Dedicated June 11, 2005. Erected by Slim Princess Chapter 395 E Clampus Vitus.

> "Near this location, on Oct. 1, 1871, escaped convicts Moses Black and Leander Morton were lynched by vigilantes to avenge the killing

of Robert Morrison, a well liked Wells Fargo agent from Benton. Morrison was a member of the Sheriff's posse who captured the convicts who had escaped form the Nevada State Penitentiary in Carson City. Following a two hour "court" proceeding the "jury" agreed that Black and Morton were guilty and they were immediately hung from a make-shift scaffold, which was quickly built during the trial."

INY 119: Look: EAST: If it is still there, isn't this a fun business name – *FedUp*.

INY 119: Note: Entering Bishop Paiute Reservation. The Paiute-Shoshone band are also known as the Owens Valley Paiute. Known as Nuumu, aka the People, they were quite industrious and creative in ways they don't get credit for. For example, they used flood irrigation from the Sierra Nevada creeks flowing down into the valley to grow native plants to sustain themselves. The only other place this occurred was with the Fremont Indians near Great Basin National Park. Later, the Anglo settlers and City of Los Angeles Dept of Water & Power used the ditches and the concept of water diversions to sustain ranches, farms, and water transport to Los Angeles. The Paiutes also made very nice cradle boards to carry their babies in and were noteworthy basket makers.

INY 119: Bishop (formerly Bishop Creek) is at an elevation of 4,150'. The population is around 3,879. The town was named after Bishop Creek, which flows down out of the Sierra Nevada. And the creek was named after Samuel Addison Bishop, a settler in the Owens Valley. The Bishop Creek Post Office operated from 1870 to 1889 and then from 1935 to 1938.

Bishop is known as the "Mule Capital of the World" and a week-long festival called Bishop Mule Days has been held since 1969 during the week of Memorial Day, celebrating the contributions of pack mules to the area.

The economy of Bishop suffered when farmers sold their land because of the water wars. Jack Foley, a Bishop resident and sound effects specialist, mitigated the economic loss by persuading several Los Angeles studio bosses that the town of Bishop would be ideal as a location to shoot westerns.

Erick Schat's Bakkerÿ is a bakery and tourist attraction in Bishop. It is known for their unique bread, called Original Sheepherder's Bread (trademarked in 1938), and produces 450 other products. The bakery bakes approximately 25,000 loaves of bread per day, and they have produced their Sheepherder's bread continuously since 1907. The bakery uses a Basque recipe. The bakery bakes the bread in stone hearth ovens, with no preservatives, and everything is handmade from scratch, including the yeast.

Scan the QR Code in the Index of Websites: **Bishop Chamber of Commerce & Visitors Bureau** for a terrific website and more information of the town and surrounding area.

At INY 116: Note: US 6 is a good alternate route through Hawthorne and Yerington when the roads are bad between Mammoth and Bridgeport. It adds roughly forty-five minutes to the trip. (But then if the roads are that bad it's probably quicker than putting on chains and doing that distance at 35 mph.)

INY 116: A: Look: WEST: At the stoplight for the turnoff to Hwy 6 is a monument to **"James D. Birchim."** Dedicated May 28, 2011. Erected by Veterans of Foreign Wars Post 8988, Bishop California.

> "A native son of the Owens Valley, James Douglas Birchim spent his childhood in Independence and graduated from high school in 1964. His college studies were guided by an avid interest in entomology but were cut short due to the Vietnam War. In February of 1966, he began his Army schooling with OCS, Jump School, Chemical Corp, and Special Forces Training. In July of 1968, he was sent to Vietnam and was assigned to MACVSOG. On a mission in Laos his team came under attack. Jim called in air strikes on top of them and requested immediate extraction as all members of the team were wounded. All men returned to Kontum except for two that were Killed in Action and Jim who continues to be listed as Missing in Action as of November 15, 1968. For his heroism, Jim was awarded the Distinguished Service Cross and Purple Heart. Above all he was a husband, father and beloved member of the Birchim family.

NO EXIT NECESSARY: RENO, NV TO ADELANTO, CA

In loving memory of all those who are still listed as Missing in Action and Prisoners of War."

NA: The Bishop Paiute Tribe, formerly known as the Paiute-Shoshone Indians of the Bishop Community of the Bishop Colony, is a federally recognized tribe of Mono and Timbisha Indians of the Owens Valley. Both the *Nuumu* (Paiute) and *Newe* (Shoshone) people descend from the *Numu*, the original people of the Valley.

In 1912, the US Government set aside 67,000 acres for the reservation, but in 1936 it was reduced to 875 acres. Today, with about 2,000 members, the Bishop Paiute Tribe is the fifth largest but on one of the smallest areas of land.

A: The **Owens Valley Paiute Shoshone Cultural Center** is a museum and gift shop with Native American crafts.

INY 109: Look: WEST: Sign for **Grand Army of the Republic Highway**. The idea was conceived by US Army Major William L. Anderson, Jr. to honor Union Civil War veterans. In April 1934, Sons of Union Veterans of the Civil War began promoting the idea. Each state had to sign a bill naming the route. California did so in 1943. The highway was formally dedicated in 1953. (Originally the road was US Route 6. In 1937 US 6 became a transcontinental highway, it ran from Long Beach, California, 3,652 miles to Provincetown on Cape Cod in Massachusetts.) For a more in-depth article *scan the QR Code in the Index of Websites:* **US 6**[1].

INY 109: A: Look: WEST: Sign erected by Caltrans Historic Highway Alignments. **"From Trail to Highway," "Old Highway 23"**, and **"El Camino Sierra."** It was during the 1870s the Good Roads Movement began a nationwide campaign to develop paved roads for rural communities. The Inyo Good Road Club lobbied and labored, literally with picks and shovels, to improve the dirt road between Big Pine and Bishop.

August 31, 1910, California Governor James Gillett officially dedicated the highway as "El Camino Sierra." A prediction made during the reporting of the dedication in the September 2, 1910 edition of the Inyo Independent is quoted

---

1. https://www.fhwa.dot.gov/infrastructure/us6.cfm

as reading, "...in years to come [El Camino Sierra] will probably be the most traveled highway in the West."

Note: These signs may have been removed for construction. (2022).

"From Trail to Highway"

"Graded dirt roads grew out of old Native American use trails. These were adequate for foot and horse traffic, as well as for the horse-drawn wagons that followed as this isolated region was settled. The local population enthusiastically promoted and often built these roads in order to establish and maintain access with the outside world, and to promote tourism, which early on was recognized as a potential source of revenue for this scenic region. The Inyo Good Road Club was established in 1910 to promote local highway construction both here and at the State Capitol in Sacramento.

With the arrival of the 20th Century automobiles began replacing horses and buggies on the local roads. It soon became clear that the old wagon roads were not adequate for automobile traffic, and that building highways was too big an enterprise for small, isolated rural communities.

In 1909 the State Legislature passed a bond issue of $18,000,000 for the acquisition and construction of a state highway system. Despite its unpopularity with urban California the bond was ratified the following year thanks to overwhelming support from rural voters.

Prior to 1920 roads in this region were built using locally hired day laborers, unlike the rest of California, where contractors were primarily used. This was considered adequate when it was generally assumed that the roads would not get the kind of traffic they now see, and it was commonly believed that the job of building roads would someday be complete.

NO EXIT NECESSARY: RENO, NV TO ADELANTO, CA

The first local highway building contract was awarded on January 19, 1920 to Chas. B. Solteras for grading US-395 (then SR-23) from Independence to Division Creek. The final cost for both grading and oiling this section of highway was $37,658. In contrast, the Blackrock Four-Lane project, which added two lanes, widened shoulders and rehabilitated existing lanes between Ft. Independence and the Poverty Hills, was completed in July 2007 at a cost of more than $31,000,000."

"Old Highway 23"

"On July 6, 1921 contract #309 was awarded to the Nevada Contracting Company to pave 11.66 miles of SR-23, the precursor to US-395, from just north of Big Pine to near Bishop. The winning bid was $126,794. The section of road angling toward the small bridge at the south end of this pullout is part of the original highway. At the far end of the section visible from here the remnant of the original highway crosses the road to Keough's Hot Springs – already a popular resort when the original highway was built.

The original highway ran along the base of the mountains rather than more directly between Bishop and Big Pine. As highways are upgraded they are often realigned, shortening the distance between major destinations while enhancing the operation of the highway.

Additional improvements to highways include widening. The original two-lane highway here was fifteen-feet wide, adequate for both the speed and volume of traffic when it was constructed. Modern roads have twelve foot wide lanes. On major highways, like US-395, the trend is to separate opposing lanes with medians whenever possible."

"El Camino Sierra"

"The modern four-lane highway here was once part of a Native American trade route linking the Owens Valley with tribes to the west via Walker Pass. Jedediah Smith may have passed this way in 1826, but the first recorded journey through the Owens Valley, paralleling what would eventually become US-395, was by Joseph Walker in 1934. Gold Rush brought prospectors into the area, and by the late 1800s the former trail had become a wagon and stage road. The road linked the local mines to the ranches, farms, and small communities that supplied them. It was called *El Camino Sierra*, and was envisioned to eventually run from Los Angeles to Reno.

While El Camino Sierra was never built in its entirety, sections were built linking local destinations. This construction was spurred by local individuals, entrepreneurs and business groups with the blessing, if not direct help, from the State. The vision of a state highway system made up of roads of the scale and ambition of the originally conceived El Camino Sierra would have to wait until the 20th Century and the rise of the automobile."

"Highway design and layout reflects both the culture and technology of the times." "This map shows the original highway between this pullout and the Poverty Hills, a few miles south of Big Pine. Note how much more direct the modern highway is compared with the original route."

"Why is that?" "Perhaps the original route followed the most passable terrain by foot or wagon. As the route evolved into a roadway the original alignment may have been sufficient for the slower vehicles of its day.

With the slower pace of travel of the period, more closely spaced destinations may have been necessary to provide services for travelers crossing the high desert terrain. Older roads directly connected more places, rather than serve as arteries, which bypass minor destinations and connect major destinations, as modern highways do.

Improvements in automobile design, efficiency and reliability may be a factor as well. Modern vehicles are capable of traveling longer distances at higher speeds, requiring less frequent stops.

Construction capabilities may have been a factor in determining the location of the original road. Older roads followed the terrain rather than plowed through it, allowing for easier construction with the equipment of the era.

As highways are realigned and upgraded they are often realigned to enhance highway operation and to accommodate the types, speeds and numbers of vehicles using the road."

INY 108: A: Keogh Hot Springs to the WEST was established in 1919. Contact Keogh Hot Springs for hours of operation and pricing.

INY 107: Note: Elevation 4000'.

INY 105: Look: EAST: **Owens Valley Radio Observatory** was established in 1956. It is owned and operated by Caltech (California Institute of Technology) as a radio astronomy observatory. The solar array portion has been operated by New Jersey Institute of Technology since 1997.

If the lake in front of the Observatory is full, one can sometimes see windsurfers whipping around out there with their colored sails.

INY 102: Look: EAST: That lineman in the field isn't real!

INY 101: A: Bristlecone Pine Information and Historic Landmark is to the EAST. Here you'll find a Veterans memorial, an excellent panorama of the mountain range to the west with names and elevations, and monument **"Westgaard Pass Toll Road."** Dedicated June 18, 1983. Erected by Slim Princess Chapter E Clampus Vitus.

"Camp Independence soldiers needed a road to Waucoba-Deep Springs. In 1873 J. S. "Scott" Broder completed this road and collected tolls until 1900. In 1913 A.L. Westgaard led an American

Automobile Assn. Tour across here. Seeking a new transcontinental route. State took over road in 1925."

A: Camping: Glacier View Campground is an Inyo County campground. *Scan the QR Code in the Index of Websites*: **Glacier View Campground** for more information.

A: Turn on CA 168 to reach the turnoff to **Ancient Bristlecone Pine Forest** twenty-four miles northwest.

INY 101: Big Pine (formerly Bigpine) is at an elevation of 3,989'. The population is about 1,756. The Big Pine Post Office first opened in 1870, closed for a time in 1877, changed its name to Bigpine in 1895, and reverted to Big Pine in 1962. It has a significant geologic feature (an earthquake scarp) related to the 1872 Lone Pine earthquake.

A notable resident from here, Norman Clyde (April 8, 1885 – December 23, 1972) was a famous mountaineer, nature photographer, and self-trained naturalist. He is well known for achieving over one hundred first ascents, many in the Sierra Nevada and Montana. He also set a speed climbing record on Mount Shasta in 1923. Clyde served as a climbing leader at Sierra Club base camps where he became known as "the pack that walks like a man" because of the huge backpacks he carried. In addition to as many as five cameras, he carried a hammer and cobbler's anvil to make field repairs to the client's boots.

Look: EAST at the south end of town: Ever so often they change the color of the beanie cap.

NA: The Big Pine Band of Owens Valley Paiute Shoshone Indians of the Big Pine Reservation is located here. The Reservation was established in 1912 and is 279 acres in size. Tribal members raise horses on tribal lands.

An interesting court case arose in Big Pine in 1924, Alice Piper was a fifteen-year-old Native American living in Big Pine in 1923. She wanted to attend Big Pine school but was denied on her ethnicity. Alice, who was the daughter of Pike and Annie Piper, sued the school district (along with six other children) claiming the state law establishing separate schools for "Indian children" and other children of Asian parentage was unconstitutional.

The State Supreme Court ruled unanimously that because Alice Piper's father was a tax-paying citizen, that Alice Piper therefore qualified as a citizen under the Dawes Act. The court did not, in fact, find that her 14th Amendment rights had been violated. Nonetheless, Alice Piper was invited as a pupil and her victory along with passage of the Indian Citizenship Act, on the same day, opened the door for herself and other Native American children to attend public schools in the state of California. Because of this, the Big Pine School District is memorialized as a major player in the constitutional battle over the rights of Native Americans to attend public schools segregated for "whites only." To read more about the case, *scan the QR Code in the Index of Websites*: **Piper vs. Big Pine.**

Look: EAST: The **Inyo Mountains** are a short, seventy miles north to south, mountain range. It separates the Owens Valley on the west side from Saline Valley over on the east side of the mountains. Wildlife in the area includes the endangered Inyo Mountains Salamander and the Desert Bighorn Sheep. At lower elevations grows creosote and sagebrush. Bristlecone pine forests are higher up. Several rare and endemic plants are adapted to the unique limestone soils of the mountains, including the cliff dweller, bristlecone cryptantha, and Inyo rock daisy.

INY 93: A: Wildlife viewing area. Watch for elk especially to the west. This elk has adapted to the sage and heat. The Tule Elk is found only in California. The herds were once so large the early explorers compared them to the buffalo herds on the Great Plains.

A: There is a tiny monument WEST **"Tule Elk."** Dedicated June 19, 2004. Erected by Slim Princess Chapter 395 E. Clampus Vitus.

> "The Tule Elk are found only in California. This subspecies of elk once roamed the vast grasslands of California's Central Valley in large herds. Early Spanish and American settlers hunted them nearly to extinction by 1870 there were only about 30 Tule Elk left.

A rancher in the San Joaquin Valley established a private refuge for this small herd while California passed legislation protecting the elk. In 1914 California Fish & Game began transplanting these animals to different locations in California. Established in 1933 with 56 animals, the Owens Valley herd is now managed at a maximum population of 490 animals.

Seen in these fields during the rutting season in late summer, older and stronger bulls select a harem of cows and defends them by fighting off other bulls. As winter turns to spring the entire herd moves into the foothills and remote canyons, where the calves are born. By early summer the herd gathers again on the valley floor in preparation for the new rutting season."

INY 93: Tinemaha Reservoir, to the EAST, was built in 1962 by damming the Owens River. You can only see the dam looking northbound. The reservoir is a migratory stop for both water and shore birds. Sometimes in winter, Tundra Swans can be seen here.

A: Tinemahah Wildlife Viewing Area. This overlook of the reservoir and surrounding area is EAST on E. Elna Road. Turn left onto the dirt road and go about a quarter of a mile to the parking lot.

INY 89: A: Look: EAST: Monument **"Charley's Butte."** Dedicated June 21, 1986. Erected by Slim Princess Chapter 395 E. Clampus Vitus.

"The low black ridge ½ mile southeast of this spot is named after Charley Tyler, a black cowboy, who died there March 7, 1863, defending the McGee Summers party from an Indian attack. His stand gave time for the besieged party to escape.

The site is also historic as the location of the first filing by the City of Los Angeles for water diversion rights in the Owens Valley on October 23, 1905."

NO EXIT NECESSARY: RENO, NV TO ADELANTO, CA

INY 88: A: Camping: Turn WEST on Taboose Creek Road, **Taboose Creek Campground** is two miles in. *Scan the QR Code in the Index of Websites*: **Taboose Creek Campground** for more information.

INY 87: A: Camping: Turn WEST on Aberdeen Road and follow the signs two miles to **Goodale Creek Campground**. *Scan the QR Code in the Index of Websites*: **Goodale Creek Campground** for more information.

INY 84: Look: WEST: If you happen to be coming through in the spring and the belly flowers are in bloom, these entire mountain slopes are such a lovely bright yellow.

INY 84: Look: Division Creek Rest Area on the EAST side of the highway. There is a good display of interpretive signs.

Note: There is an Electric Vehicle Charging Station located here.

The **Owens River Gorge** is a steep ten-mile canyon. Among other things, it is a popular rock- climbing destination.

Tho it begins many miles north of here, you can now start seeing the **Owens River**. It is approximately 183-miles long. The river ends at Owens Lake south of Lone Pine.

In the early 1900s the Owens River was the focus of the California Water Wars, fought between the city of Los Angeles and the inhabitants of Owens Valley over the construction of the Los Angeles Aqueduct. Since 1913, the Owens River has been diverted to Los Angeles, causing the ruin of the valley's economy and the drying of Owens Lake. In winter 2006, the Los Angeles Department of Water and Power restored five percent of the pre-aqueduct flow to the river, by court order, allowing the Owens River Gorge, the river bed in the valley, and Owens Lake to contain a small amount of water.

INY 82: A: Interpretive signs EAST at Black Rock Springs Road tell the story of the **Lower Owens River Project** presented by City of Los Angeles Department of Water and Power and the County of Inyo. There is a small monument dedicated to the memory of V.E. "Johnny" Johnson for his efforts in gaining cooperation between Los Angeles and Inyo County.

INY 77: NA: Fort Independence Reservation is home to Fort Independence Community of Paiute Indians. The reservation was established in 1915 and is 234 acres in size today.

INY 76: A: WEST: **Mt. Whitney Fish Hatchery.** Some activities include a feeding pond. In its day, the hatchery produced up to 2,000,000 fish per year.

INY 76: A: EAST: What is left of **Camp Independence Historic Site** is a monument near the corner of Schabbell Lane and Oak Creek Road.

INY 74: Independence is at an elevation of 3,930'. It became the county seat of Inyo County in 1866 when its chief competitor for the honor, a mining camp called Kearsarge, disappeared under an avalanche. The first Post Office was also established that year. A few years before that, 1861, Charles Putnam founded a trading post at the site. It became known as Putnam's, and later Little Pine from the Little Pine Creek.

Independence is a popular resupply stop for hikers trekking the 2,650-mile Pacific Crest Trail, which extends from the Mexican border to Canada along the crest of the Sierra Nevada and Cascade Range. The highest pass along the entire trail, 13,153' Forester Pass, is directly west of Independence. (An excellent book to read about a woman who hiked the trail is *Cheryl Strayed*.)

The 1997 film *Trial and Error* was filmed here. It is a lawyer comedy starring Charlize Theron and Jeff Daniels.

A: The **Eastern California Museum** is located on Grant Street. The museum has over 15,550 records in its database of various collections. About 27,000 historic photographs are housed there also, the majority are from the late 1800s through the 1950s.

A brochure is available for a historic walking tour of the town.

RA: WEST: **Independence County Park** and **Rest Area.**

INY 68: Manzanar National Historic Site is the site of one of ten American internment camps in the United States. During World War II, from December

NO EXIT NECESSARY: RENO, NV TO ADELANTO, CA

1942 to 1945, over 110,000 Japanese-Americans were forcibly removed from their homes and incarcerated.

Manzanar (which means "apple orchard" in Spanish) was identified by the United States National Park Service as the best-preserved of the former camp sites, and preserves and interprets the legacy of Japanese-American incarceration in the United States. It has been thoughtfully designed and presented in a straightforward manner.

Since the end of World War II, there has been debate over the terminology used to refer to Manzanar, and the other camps in which Americans of Japanese ancestry and their immigrant parents were incarcerated by the Government during the war. Manzanar has been referred to as a "War Relocation Center," "relocation camp," "relocation center," "internment camp", and "concentration camp", and the controversy over which term is the most accurate and appropriate continues to the present day.

Long before the first incarcerees arrived in March 1942, Manzanar was home to Native Americans who lived mostly in villages near several creeks in the area. Ranchers and miners formally established the town of Manzanar in 1910, but abandoned the town by 1929 after the City of Los Angeles purchased the water rights to virtually the entire area. As different as these groups were, their histories displayed a common thread of forced relocation.

Note: For more information while driving by tune your radio to 1610 AM.

INY 64: A: The monument **"The Alabama Gates."** Dedicated June 27, 1992. Erected by Slim Princess Chapter #395 E Clampus Vitus.

> "The Alabama Gates and gate house were constructed in 1913 when the Los Angeles Aqueduct was built to dewater the aqueduct when maintenance is necessary. On November 16, 1924, seventy or more local citizens seized the aqueduct at the Alabama Gates and diverted the city's water supply through the gates into the dry Owens River to publicize the concerns of Owens Valley residents. Four days later the water was voluntarily allowed to again flow into the aqueduct. Over the years, attempts to reconcile the city's water needs and

the concerns of valley residents have moved from confrontation to negotiation."

Controversy surrounded the diversion of water by the city of Los Angeles from the beginning. In November 1927, a group of armed ranchers seized the Alabama Gates and dynamited part of the system, letting water return to the Owens River. This brought the plight of the valley to the nation's awareness. Then in November 1931 the Los Angeles Times reported, "Sunday night's blast touched off on the Grape Vine siphon marked the eighth actual dynamiting of the Owens Valley Aqueduct system in a series of outrages directed against the city's water supply system outside the city of Los Angeles.

INY 63: Look: WEST: Alabama Spillway was built in 1913. They fly both the US and POW flags. When the wind blows and they are snapping in the breeze it's a pretty grand sight.

INY 60: Warning: Begin 55-mph speed limit.

INY 59: A: A sign, **"Grave of 1872 Earthquake Victims"** Historical Landmark No. 507, points uphill to a mass grave. The monument on the fence surrounding the last resting site of those killed reads:

> **"Disaster in 1872"**
>
> "On the date of March 26, 1872, an earthquake of major proportions shook Owens Valley and nearly destroyed the town of Lone Pine.
>
> Twenty seven persons were killed.
>
> In addition to single burials, 16 of the victims were interred in a common grave enclosed by this fence."

A memorial erected by the Lion's Club reads:

> **"March 26, 1988"**

NO EXIT NECESSARY: RENO, NV TO ADELANTO, CA

"116 years ago this date, an 8.3 earthquake hit Lone Pine. 27 people died. Sixteen are buried at this site in a common grave. Alice Meysan age 11, (family still resides in Independence) Manuel Ybaceta Anotonia Montoya, Maria Tarrazona & her children. The rest of French, Irish, Chilean, Mexican & Native American ancestry are known but to God. March 26, 1872"

INY 58: A: Just before entering the town on the WEST is a sign before a majestic, sprawling oak tree. This is provided courtesy of Southern Inyo Womens Club and informs the passerby:

"This English pedunculate Oak tree originated in Sherwood Forest England. Around the turn of the [20th] century a small sprout was sent to Lone Pine. A member of the Fred French family planted the sprout on this original site, a part of the Old Harvey Ranch."

INY 58: Lone Pine is at an elevation of 3,727'. From possible choices of urban, rural, and frontier, the Census Bureau identifies this area as "frontier."

A cabin was built here during the winter of 1861–62. A settlement developed over the following two years. The Lone Pine Post Office opened in 1870.

On March 26, 1872, at 2:30 AM, Lone Pine experienced a violent earthquake that destroyed most of the town. At the time, the town consisted of eighty buildings made of mud and adobe; only twenty structures were left standing. As a result of the quake, which formed Diaz Lake, a total of twenty-six of the near 300 residents lost their lives. One of the few remaining structures predating the earthquake is the 21"-thick "Old Adobe Wall" located in the alley behind La Florista, a flower shop.

In 1920, the history of Lone Pine was dramatically altered when a movie production company came to the Alabama Hills, to the west of town, to make the silent film *The Roundup*. Other companies soon discovered the scenic location, and in the coming decades, over 400 films, 100 television episodes, and countless commercials have used Lone Pine and the Alabama Hills as a film location.

J. BUTLER KYLE

A: Lone Pine Film History Museum was founded in 2006. The museum collects, preserves, and exhibits a broad and diverse collection of western film memorabilia associated with the American western film genre as well as others. In and around the area of Lone Pine and the Alabama Hills, over 400 films and over 1,000 commercials have been recorded. Hollywood first came on location in in 1920, using the unique scenery of the area. In October of 1990, the first Lone Pine Film Festival was held to celebrate all this movie history including tours of the location's movies were filmed at. *Scan the QR Code in the Index of Websites:* **Lone Pine Film History Museum** for more information.

Note: Behind the museum are eight electric vehicle charging stations.

A: Southern Inyo Museum is located at 127 W. Bush Street.

NA: The **Lone Pine Paiute-Shoshone Reservation** is a federally recognized tribe. The reservation was established through a land exchange between the City of Los Angeles and the Department of Interior on April 20, 1937. The Reservation covers a little over 237 acres.

Look: WEST: **Mount Whitney** is the highest summit in the contiguous United States and the Sierra Nevada, with an elevation of 14,505'.

INY 55: A: EAST: The **Eastern Sierra Visitor Center** is on the corner at CA 136 towards Death Valley.

A: This approximate thirty-five-mile loop along CA 136 to CA 190 runs around the east side of Owens Lake. It ties back to US 395 near Olancha at INY 35. The loop takes you by the town of Keeler (that had a population in the 1870s of 5,000 people), once a shipping port for the Cerro Gordo Mines; past monuments to the Dolomite Mine, Keeler, and Owen Lake Silver Lead Furnace; interpretive signs for Owens Lake Dust Mitigation; mining ruins, and other abandoned sites.

INY 55: A: In 1872, the Lone Pine earthquake dropped Owens Valley about 20' and opened up a spring that filled the lowland creating **Diaz Lake**. Today the lake covers eighty acres. More than a decade earlier, Rafael and Eleuterio

Diaz emigrated from Chile and established a cattle ranch here. They sold the land to the City of Los Angeles.

Camping: *Scan the QR Code in the Index of Websites:* **Diaz Lake Campground** for more information.

INY 42: Owens Lake is mostly a dry lake bed, but it wasn't always this way. Until 1913, the lake held a significant amount of water, up to twelve miles long and eight miles wide. When Los Angeles diverted Owens River, by 1926 the lake had dried up. Through court orders, some of the river now runs back into the lake.

As far back as 1905, the lake was thought to be "excessively saline." Today, the large salt flat is made of a mixture of clay, sand, and a variety of minerals. After the rains come and hot summer days where the ground temperature exceeds 150°, the minerals create a chemical soup in the form of a muddy brine pond. If conditions are especially right, the salty lakebed can bloom bright pink after a halophilic, or salt-loving, archaea (single-celled organisms) spread. But more commonly the winds stir up noxious alkali dust storms that carry away as much as 4,000,000 tons of dust from the lakebed each year. Since 2013, the dry Owens Lake is considered the largest single source of dust pollution in the United States. This can cause respiratory problems as the dust caries carcinogens such as cadmium, nickel, and arsenic.

In 2018, Owens Lake was awarded a Western Hemisphere Shorebird Reserve Network site. There are only 104 of these areas from Alaska to South America. Over one hundred species of birds visit the lake in their annual migrations.

Owens Lake was named after Richard Owens, he was a guide for explorer John C. Frémont.

For a couple of great websites of information, stories, and much, much more *scan the QR Codes in the Index of Websites* for **Owens Valley History,** or **Owens Lake and surrounding area.** But *scan the QR Codes in the Index of Websites* for a fun **Owens Lake Sea Monster Tale.**

J. BUTLER KYLE

Look: EAST: On an old map, those abandoned industrial ruins are where the railroad siding of Bartlett was. It was Pittsburgh Plate Glass Company's chemical plant used up until the 1960s, when they ceased crystallizing and processing carbonate compounds mined from the dry lake bed.

INY 45: A: The **Cottonwood Charcoal Kilns**, are EAST down a dirt and gravel road about a mile. Two of the traditional stone masonry "beehive" charcoal kilns are there. They were built to transform wood from the trees in Cottonwood Canyon above the lake into charcoal. This was fed into the Cerro Gordo mines' silver and lead smelters across the lake at Swansea.

A: **"Charcoal Cottonwood Kilns"** monument is located EAST at the beginning of the dirt road to the kilns. "[The] Plaque originally dedicated in 1955 by the California Eastern Sierra Museum Association. Plaque stolen in 1970. Recovered by Inyo County Sheriff's Dept. Rededicated May 15, 1976." Erected by Slim Princess Chapter No. 395 E Clampus Vitus.

> "In June 1873 Colonel Sherman Stevens built a sawmill and flume on Cottonwood Creek high in the Sierras directly west of this spot. The flume connected with the Los Angeles Bullion Road. The lumber from the flume was used for timbering in the mine and buildings, and the wood was turned into charcoal in these kilns, then hauled to Steven's wharf east of here on Owens Lake. There it was put on the steamer the "Bessie Brady," or the "Mollie Stevens," hauled directly across the land, and from there wagons took it up the "Yellow Grade" to Cerro Gordo mine, high in the Inyo Mountains above Keeler. M. W. Belshaw's furnaces had used all available wood around the Cerro Gordo and this charcoal was necessary to continued production.
>
> The bullion which was then taken out by the reverse of this route was hauled to Los Angeles on Remi Nadeau's 14, 16, 18 animal freight wagons and played a major part in the building of that little pueblo into the city of today."

INY 41: Warning: End four-lane highway and begin 55-mph speed limit.

NO EXIT NECESSARY: RENO, NV TO ADELANTO, CA

INY 37: Cartago (formerly Carthage, Daniersburg, and Lakeville) is at an elevation of 3,629'. Located near the now abandoned settlement of Carthage, Cartago took its name from the Spanish name for ancient Carthage. The first Post Office opened in 1918.

During the heyday of mining in the area (the 1870s), Cartago was the western steamboat port for the Cerro Gordo Mines. Much of the freight it carried was silver and lead bullion. The twenty-mule team teamsters would haul the refined bars to Los Angeles, a long, trying three-week journey. After the "Bessie Brady", a barge-like vessel, launched in 1872 it cut the three-day journey around the lake down to three hours.

Scan the QR Code in the Index of Websites: **Ghost Towns** for pictures and interesting stories of Cartago and the area. At the website, *select* state: California, *click* on: Southern Region; then *click* on: Inyo. The left side of the map is all US 395 with many other sites to read about.

A: The **"Cartago Boat Landing"** monument is on the EAST side of the highway. Dedicated June 10, 1978. Erected by Slim Princess Chapter 395 E Clampus Vitus.

> "In the 1870's bullion bars from Cerro Gordo mines were hauled across Owens Lake on the steamer "Bessie Brady" to Cartago Boat Landing. Remi Nadeau's 14 mule teams hauled the bullion to Los Angeles, returning with freight."

INY 37: Look: EAST: Wouldn't you love to peek inside that yellow-orange beany cap building and maybe get a picture with T-Rex!

INY 35: Olancha (formerly Olanche) is at an elevation of 3,658'. The first Post Office opened in 1870 and still operates today. Crystal Geyser Natural Alpine Spring Water has a major bottling plant here. To the east of town lie some sand dunes, as well as a hot spring known as "Dirty Socks." *Scan the QR Code in the Index of Websites:* **Ghost Towns** for pictures and interesting stories of Olancha and the area. At the website, *select* state: California, *click* on: Southern Region; then *click* on: Inyo. The left side of the map is all US 395 with many other sites to read about.

Olancha was established by Minnard Farley, who came to the area in 1860 and discovered silver in the Coso Range. The name "Olancha" is believed to be derived from the nearby Yaudanche tribe. Farley built a stamp mill just south of Olancha Creek. The remains of a stone wall from this mill still exists.

On August 11, 1969 Manson Family members Charles "Tex" Watson and Dianne "Snake" Lake settled down in Olancha two days after Watson had stabbed Sharon Tate to death. Lake was temporarily taken into custody in Independence after complaints from Olancha residents about her swimming nude. After a few weeks the two of them left Olancha for the final Manson hideout in Death Valley.

INY 35: A: Monument on the WEST side of the highway at the intersection with CA 190 to Death Valley, **doesn't have anything on it!**

This almost thirty-five-mile loop road, CA 190 to CA 136, returns to US 395 at INY 55 near Lone Pine. It travels by the near-ghost town of Keeler; past monuments to the Dolomite Mine, Keeler, and Owen Lake Silver Lead Furnace; interpretive signs for Owens Lake Dust Mitigation; mining ruins, and other abandoned sites.

INY 34: A: The monument **"Farley's Olancha Mill"** is WEST. Plaque placed by the California State Park Commission in cooperation with the Southern Inyo Chamber of Commerce, January 30, 1965. California registered Historical Landmark No. 796.

> "M.H. Farley, working for the Silver Mountain Mining company in the Coso Mountains, conceived the idea in 1860 of building a processing mill on a creek flowing into Owens Lake. He explored and named Olancha Pass that year, and completed the first mill and furnace in the Owens River valley by December of 1862. It was located on Olancha Creek about one mile west of this marker."

INY 33: Look: WEST: See the Joshua trees and funky statues? For a great story and pictures s*can the QR Code in the Index of Websites:* **Joshua trees and funky statues** to check out Josh's blog.

NO EXIT NECESSARY: RENO, NV TO ADELANTO, CA

Joshua trees (*Yucca brevifolia*) begin to be spotted starting along here. They only grow between this elevation and up to 7000'. But they grow beyond the edges of the Mojave Desert in all compass directions despite popular view.

Mormon's are credited with giving *Yucca brevifolia* the common name Joshua tree on one of their journeys across the Mojave Desert in the mid-1800s. Seems the wide-open outstretched branches of the tree made them think of the Biblical Joshua welcoming them to the Promised Land.

INY 33: Grant was once a small community a mile and a half south of Olancha. A market, gas station, and hotel once served weary travelers trekking up or down US 395. Pack trips could be taken from trailhead points west of the community into the headwaters of the Kern River on the west side of the Sierra crest. A few old buildings are the only reminder that Grant once existed. The Highway Department removed the highway sign for Grant but then put it back up.

<u>Scan the QR Code in the Index of Websites</u>: **Ghost Towns** for pictures and interesting stories of Grant and the area. At the website, s*elect* state: <u>California</u>, <u>click</u> on: <u>Southern Region</u>; then <u>click</u> on: <u>Inyo</u>. The left side of the map is all US 395 with many other sites to read about.

INY 32: Note: Begin four-lane highway.

INY 30: Warning: High wind warning sign may be flashing. If it is, the wind can kick you around all the way to Pearsonville.

INY 24: Look: EAST: Haiwee Reservoir sparkles in the distance. Haiwee (formerly McGuire's, Hawaii and Hayways) is located on the Southern Pacific Railroad twenty-four miles south-southwest of Keeler, at an elevation of 4,075'. The settlement there began in 1864, as a way stop at Haiwai Meadows on the road between Visalia and the Owens Valley. The stop was run by a man named McGuire and his wife and young son.

While McGuire was away on January 1, 1865, his wife and son were killed in an Indian attack. In the Owens Lake Massacre, January 6, 1865, Owens Valley settler militia avenged their deaths with an attack on the Indian village where the killers had taken refuge. This was one of the last fights in the Owens Valley Indian War.

The original settlement site and the Haiwai Meadows are under the water of the Haiwee Reservoir. The town moved to a site west of the reservoir. A Post Office operated at Haiwee from 1906 to 1913.

INY 26: Note: Elevation 4000'.

INY 15: Look: Through here in the spring, the proud little orange mallow flowers line the highway on both sides for dozens and dozens of miles.

INY 21: Dunmovin (formerly Cowan Station) is at an elevation of 3,507'. A Post Office operated here from 1938 to 1941. The place was originally called Cowan Station in honor of homesteader James Cowan. Cowan Station was a freight station from the Cerro Gordo Mines to Los Angeles. When Cowan sold out in 1936, the name was changed to Dunmovin. It was a roadside service station, cafe, and store.

INY 18: Coso Junction (formerly Coso) is in Rose Valley at an elevation of 3,386'. Coso Jct. **Rest Area** is across the highway EAST. There is a nice array of interpretive signs provided by Eastern Sierra Scenic Byway – **"The March of 1863"**, **"Tule Elk in the Owens Valley"**, **"Desert Reptiles"**, and **"Nature's Cleanup Crew."** In the Coso language, it means *dove*.

The Coso Geothermal Site is located within the Coso Volcanic fields.

Note: EAST: There is an Electric Vehicle charging station.

INY 15: Look: WEST: See the ruins of someone's dream? I always wonder what their story is.

INY 13: A: Fossil Falls is a dry waterfall formed 10,000 to 20,000 years ago by glaciers and Owens River flooding in the basaltic lava field. It is otherworldly and magnificent.

Turn EAST on Cinder Road and go about a mile down the gravel lane. There is a small parking lot, and the trail to the falls is very rough. Eastern Sierra Scenic

NO EXIT NECESSARY: RENO, NV TO ADELANTO, CA

Byways erected several interpretive signs: Fossil Falls **"Sculpted by Fire and Water"**, Fossil Dry Falls **"Window to the Past"**, and Early People at Fossil Falls **"Life at the Edge of Volcanoes and Glaciers."**

A good read with some nice pictures on the ancient waterfall can be found by <u>scanning the QR Code in the Index of Websites</u>: **Fossil Falls**.

INY 11: Look: EAST: **Little Lake** is a bird refuge along the Owens Valley Corridor of the Pacific Flyway. Each year thousands of birds stop off at the lake during their spring and fall migration. When the sun hits the lake just right, the water can be dazzling.

INY 10: This is the end of the Eastern Sierra Scenic Byway. Elevation 3000'.

INY 4: Look: EAST: The other side of that far ridgeline is Death Valley.

INY 0: Pearsonville is essentially a ghost town. The 2000 census had a population of twenty-seven, down to seventeen in 2010, but 2019 showed only seven people lived here. It is however, still dubbed the "Hubcap Capital of the World" because of resident Lucy Pearson's collection of hubcaps. At one time it was rumored there were over 80,000 of them.

Look: WEST: You must look carefully through the creosote bushes to see the hub caps, but they are there behind the chain-link fence.

There is a book written by mother Lucy and daughter Janice Pearson that tells the story of how Pearsonville was established. You can google the title *Pearsonville, Ca 93527 (The True Story of the Pearson Family – Against All Odds)* for available retailers.

A: The statue of the **Uniroyal Girl** is on the EAST side of the highway. This 18', 230-pound statue was originally built in the 1960s by International Fiberglass. There are only two of the Uniroyal Girls in California. By 1970, the International Fiberglass catalog offered her as "Miss America" for $3,150 dressed in a simple bikini. The clothes option cost more. This Uniroyal Girl is known as "Hubcap Lady."

J. BUTLER KYLE

For a quick article, *Scan the QR Code in the Index of Websites:* **Pearsonville**, Hubcap Capital of the World. For a terrific article on the many and various Muffler Man and Uniroyal Girls *scan the QR Code in the Index of Websites:* **Uniroyal Girls.** Once there, scroll down the alphabetical page, and you will get to Pearsonville and Hubcap Lady's story.

NO EXIT NECESSARY: RENO, NV TO ADELANTO, CA

Kern County, California

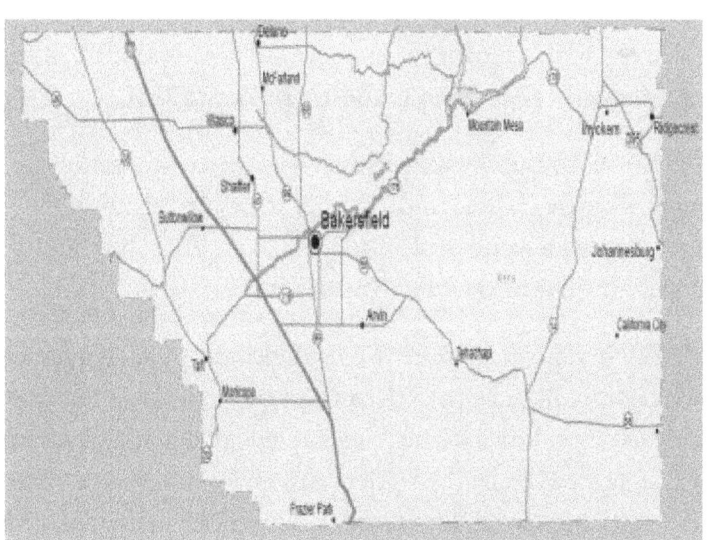

KER 37: Kern County [Milepost Sign designated as **KER**] spans the southern end of the Central Valley. At 8,161 square miles, it is a little larger than the state of Massachusetts with a population of around 909,000. It ranges west to the southern slope of the Coast Range and east beyond the southern slope of the eastern Sierra Nevada into the Mojave Desert. However, US 395 only travels 37 miles through the County.

The county's economy is heavily linked to agriculture as well as petroleum extraction. (That orchard off to the east is pistachios.) There is a strong aviation, space, and military presence, such as Edwards Air Force Base, the China Lake Naval Air Weapons Station, and Mojave Air and Space Port. The county suffers from significant water supply issues and poor air quality.

The county's name is from the Kern River, which was named after Edward Kern, a cartographer for General John C. Frémont's 1845 expedition, which crossed Walker Pass to the west. The Kern River was originally named Rio Bravo de San Felipe by missionary and explorer Father Francisco Garces when he explored the area in 1776.

KER 32: Look: WEST: That single Joshua tree by the ratty, old shack is made of horseshoes.

KER 29: Warning: End four-lane highway and two-lane begins. US 395 continues south but you must veer left off the present course toward San Bernardino. **Please drive with caution from here to Kramer Jct., many people become impatient and pass when it doesn't seem prudent.**

INY 17: A: Turnoff EAST to the town of **Ridgecrest** where the Maturango Museum, Death Valley Tourist Center, and Northern Mojave Visitor Center are located. Ridgecrest also has a wonderful Petroglyph Park. There is an annual Petroglyph Festival held the first weekend in November.

KER 24: Look: WEST: **Inyokern Airport (FAA Identifier: IYK)** is a public use airport at 2,457' elevation. In years past, the airport was used as a drag strip, glider operations and has a film history. The drag strip opened in 1954 but was closed in 2005 because of new Federal Aviation Administration regulations. Also starting in the 1950s, regular glider records were set out of Inyokern in various aerial equipment. Many well-known pilots have flown gliders out of there, including Neil Armstrong and Steve Fossett. After the drag strip was closed the Ridgecrest Regional Film Commission began promoting the airport. This is where the Lexus IS air drop was filmed.

Remember the earlier mention of a pistachio orchard at mile marker KER 37? *Scan the QR Code in the Index of Websites:* **Inyokern Airport and Pistachio controversy** to read a 2013 news article about reported concerns over the planned eighty-acre orchard and the airport.

KER 24: Inyokern (formerly Siding 16 and Magnolia) is to the WEST. Its name came from being near the border between Inyo and Kern Counties. The town is at an elevation of 2,434'.

Founded in the mid-19th century, Inyokern was a small agricultural community. The town expanded during construction of the Owens Valley aqueduct. The first Post Office opened in 1910.

NO EXIT NECESSARY: RENO, NV TO ADELANTO, CA

The Department of the Navy originally located its new warfare center here at the beginning of World War II. That's why the runways are so long. The military base was subsequently moved to the east twelve miles and the city of Ridgecrest was born as a commercial support center for that Base.

Inyokern has the highest insolation (exposure to the sun's rays and the amount of solar radiation reaching a given area) of any location on the North American continent. There are over 365 days of sunshine each year.

Visible to the SOUTHWEST, the **El Paso Mountains** are in the northern Mojave Desert. The Coso People were early Native American's who inhabited this region. They created extensive petroglyphs within the El Paso and neighboring mountains, and conducted considerable trade with other tribes as distant as the Chumash on the Pacific coast.

Welcome to the northern most fringe of the **Mojave Desert.** This is an arid rain-shadow desert and the driest desert in North America. At only 47,877 square miles, it is the smallest of the North American deserts.

The Mojave Desert is bordered by the Great Basin Desert to the north and the Sonoran Desert to the south and east. The Tehachapi Mountains delineate its western boundary, while the San Gabriel Mountains and San Bernardino Mountains border it to the south. The mountain boundaries are distinct because they are outlined by the two largest faults in California – the San Andreas and Garlock faults. Elevations above 2,000' in the Mojave are commonly referred to as the High Desert; but Death Valley is the lowest elevation in North America at -280', yes below sea level, and is one of the Mojave Desert's more notorious places.

The spelling Mojave originates from the Spanish language. The alternate spelling Mohave comes from modern English. Both are used today. The word is a shortened form of *Hamakhaave*, their endonym, or self-designated name, in their native language, which means "beside the water."

KER 14: Look: EAST: That fellow has spent considerable time creating that little oasis. I wonder if out his back door is a mine?

KER 14: Look: WEST: Did you see the stone sculpture of the man holding the American flag?

KER 14: Warning: Begin 5% climb.

KER 14: Look: EAST: This is the Spangle Off Highway Vehicle (OHV) area. Especially over holiday weekends, there are lots of Off-Highway Vehicles and large RV camps.

KER 14: Warning: Begin 5% three-mile downgrade: Elevation 3509'.

KER 4: Warning: Short, steep run. Railroad crossing at the bottom is *not* exempt. Although we have never seen a train be aware.

KER 4: Warning: Climb-out southbound with limited passing lanes. Elevation 3000'.

KER 1: A: To the WEST on Redrock-Randsburg Road is **Randsburg** (formerly Rand Camp). Today it is considered a living ghost town. But back in 1895, gold was discovered at Rand Mine near here. The first Post Office opened soon after in 1896. A mining camp quickly formed and was named Rand Camp. Both the mine and the camp were named after the gold mining region in South Africa. Randsburg is at an elevation of 3,504'.

Scattered through town are several monuments and pictures of its origins, as well as the old city jail site, historic Fiddler's Gulch, mining relics, and Randsburg Desert Museum. Scan the QR Code in the Index of Websites: **Randsburg Desert Museum** for a good website of information on the towns in the area, the claims and many mines, and so much more. Click on the various headings across the top banner for each town.

In 1989, country singer Dwight Yoakam filmed his video for *Long White Cadillac* in town.

KER 1: Look: EAST: Mines of yesteryear and even today dot the hillside.

NO EXIT NECESSARY: RENO, NV TO ADELANTO, CA

KER 0: Johannesburg is in the mining district of the Rand Mountains. It is at an elevation of 3,517'. The town is often called "Jo-burg" by locals and frequent visitors to the area.

During the first half of the 20th century, the Rand Mining District was the main gold producing region of California. Johannesburg grew to support mining operation at Randsburg. Mining centered on the Yellow Aster Mine, which was discovered in 1894. In 1919, on Red Mountain, the Rand Silver Mine was founded. The Rand Mine produced more silver than any mine in California. From 1897 to 1933, the end of the Randsburg Railway was here.

Johannesburg was named by miners who had previously worked in the gold region of South Africa. The first Post Office at Johannesburg opened in 1897.

For a historic overview of the town, *scan the QR Code in the Index of Websites*: **Ghost Towns.** At the website, *select* state: California, *click* on: Southern Region; then *click* on: Kern. On the far right, in the middle, you'll see Johannesburg (and Randsburg too). Then click on the community you want to read about.

J. BUTLER KYLE

San Bernardino County, California

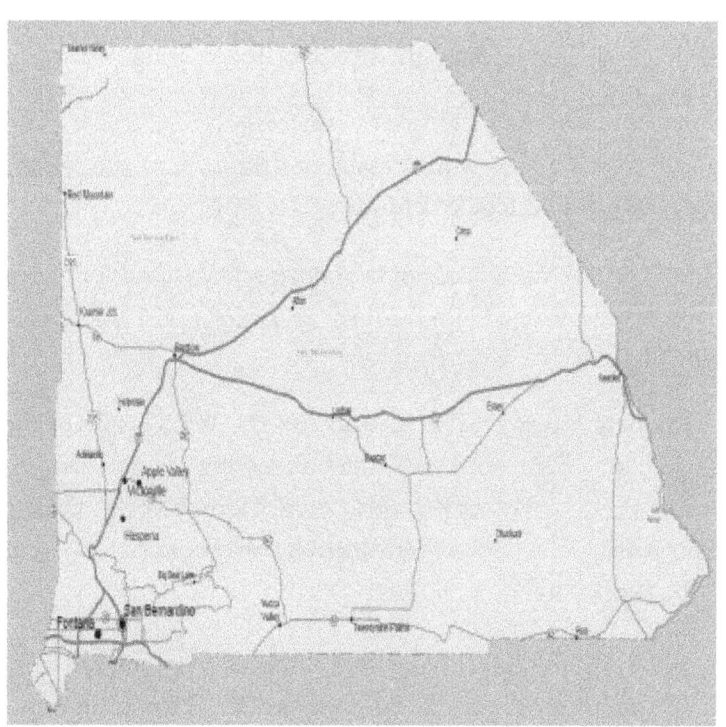

SBD 73: San Bernardino County [Milepost Sign designated as **SBD**] is officially known as County of San Bernardino. It is the 5th-most populous county in California at over 2,181,000. The county seat is in the city of San Bernardino. It was the Franciscans who gave the name San Bernardino to a snowcapped peak in Southern California, in honor of the saint, and thus from him the county was so named. San Bernardino County is also known as the Inland Empire. With an area of 20,105 square miles, San Bernardino County is the largest county in the United States by area, although some of Alaska's boroughs and census areas are larger. It is slightly larger than the states of New Jersey, Connecticut, Delaware, and Rhode Island combined, and larger than seventy different sovereign nations. US 395 travels 73 miles through San Bernardino County.

J. BUTLER KYLE

Note: San Bernardino County has emergency call boxes along the way. They are mostly on the EAST side of the road and at about every two miles.

SBD 72: Red Mountain (formerly known as Osdick) is at 3400' elevation. The Post Office opened under the name Osdick in 1922 and changed its name to Red Mountain in 1929. Red Mountain is part of the mining district of Randsburg and Johannesburg.

A billboard used to advertise *coldcockwhiskey.com*. For a fun review, *scan the QR Code in the Index of Websites*: **Coldcock Whiskey.**

Note: Owl Spy Shop is on the WEST side of the highway and sounds perfectly intriguing. For pictures of the inside (as of 2021) *Scan the QR Code in the Index of Websites*: **Owl Spy Shop.**

A: Historic sign **"Historic Silver Dollar Saloon"** on the WEST side of the highway. The sign was erected by the following organizations: www.GoldProspectors.org, www.oc49er.com, www.ProspectorsClub.org, www.TaftProspectors.com, www.RedMtnKellySilver.com, and www.RandDesertMuseum.com.

> "In 1919 the famous Kelly Silver Mine was discovered up the hill and in the same year, the Silver Dollar Saloon opened. This was one of the first saloons to open during the silver boom. The Rand Mining District had three booms – Gold in Randsburg, Tungsten in Atolia, and the third here in Red Mountain when On April 12, 1919, the discovery of the silver ore bodies was made by Jack Nosser and W. H. Williams. Later it was worked by the California Rand Silver Mine.
>
> The Silver Dollar was a speakeasy during Prohibition and for a period of time, the entire highway here was lined with brothels, gambling houses and saloons. Originally, the Silver Dollar opened as 'The Northern' in 1919. The name was changed to the Silver Dollar in the 1930s. (As a footnote, names like; The Silver Dollar, The Gold Nugget, The Owl and others were popular names of old west saloons).

NO EXIT NECESSARY: RENO, NV TO ADELANTO, CA

The Silver Dollar was one of 30 saloons operating here in Red Mountain. At the time, the Kelly Silver Mine was the richest silver ore in the United States, so this town was really hoppin' with hundreds of miners and later, many came to share in the mineral wealth."

A: Historic sign **"Santa Fe Silver Mine"** on the WEST side of the highway. The sign was erected by the following organizations: www.GoldProspectors.org, www.oc49er.com, www.ProspectorsClub.org, www.TaftProspectors.com, www.RedMtnKellySilver.com, and www.RandDesertMuseum.com.

"After the famous Kelly Silver Mine was discovered down the road, many other rich veins of silver were discovered in the surrounding area and the Santa Fe Silver Mine was one of them! (A considerable amount of gold was also extracted from this ore) The vein was worked and timbered to almost 1000' down.

In 1924, the Santa Fe Group had comprised 15 claims and is in the town of Osdick (now Red Mountain) on the Kramer-Johannesburg branch of the Santa Fe Railroad. It adjoined the California Rand Silver property on the northeast. The owners: Wortley Consolidated Mines Company; C. C. Wortley, president.

February 13, 1925: "RICH STRIKE OF EIGHTEEN-FOOT LEDGE RUBY SILVER AND $40 GOLD ORE IN SANTA FE MINE SATURDAY. Saturday last the working crew in the Santa Fe mine at Osdick uncovered a rich ledge of ruby ore carrying some $40.00 in gold on their 935-foot level and since that time the reports are that the ledge is 18 feet wide. This is indeed good news for the Rand Mining District, but new that has been daily for the past several months.

This discovery will give to the district another producer that is likely to equal the California Rand Silver in richness.

Two or three months ago the ore was just uncovered, but it was accomplished with so much water that the months between the find and the development of it as far as it has gone, had to be spent in finding a way to get rid of the water. A few days ago the new pumps installed in the mine unwatered the shaft and the ledge was uncovered sufficiently to tell the glad news that another mine had been found in the celebrated Rand Mining District. – **Randsburg Times"**

SBD 69: A: "Historic Atolia and the Stringer District." The sign was erected by the following organizations: www.GoldProspectors.org, www.oc49er.com, www.ProspectorsClub.org, www.TaftProspectors.com, www.RedMtnKellySilver.com, and www.RandDesertMuseum.com.

"Since 1896 miners and prospectors in the Stringer District (southeast of Randsburg) had been cursing the unwanted appearance of the creamy white substance in their pans and dry washers that was interfering with the gold recover. The nasty stuff was nicknamed "heavy spar." The Stringer District was so named because of the many rich gold quartz stringers.

Around 1904 is when that 'nasty white stuff' that was previously tossed out was discovered to be scheelite, the ore of tungsten – (with the Papoose Mine discovery and the later location of the Union Mine.) The Papoose was the leading scheelite min in the world! Randsburg had something to shout about again. Her second boom was on! In later years, the price of tungsten dropped and it was imported cheaper from China. The famous Mojave Gold Nugget was reportedly found a couple of miles from here by Ty Paulsen in 1977 while he was metal detecting. A replica is up the road at the Owl Café/Museum (701 Highway 395) in Red Mountain. The original is at the Los Angeles County Natural History Museum along with many other beautiful Gold Rush nuggets that they have as part of their collection. You can also Google 'Mojave Nugget' for more information on it."

NO EXIT NECESSARY: RENO, NV TO ADELANTO, CA

SBD 69: Look: Although you entered the Mojave Desert several miles back, now it presents itself in its majesty here before you.

SBD 68: Look: To the farthest horizon south and east. Those are the mountains beyond Lucerne Valley and up to Big Bear Ski Area in the San Bernardino Mountains.

SBD 67: Warning: Daylight Headlight Section.

SBD 46: Kramer Junction (also known as Four Corners) is an intersection at US 395 and CA 58. Both food and fuel are available.

Kramer Junction came in to being as a railroad siding where Southern Pacific Railroad intersected with Randsburg Railroad. Two miles west of here was the abandoned community of Kramer, so named after the Southern Pacific Railroad employee, a German native, Miritz Kramer, in 1882.

According to the Southern California Earthquake Data Center, the 6.2-mile-long Kramer Hills Fault runs from here south to Kramer Hills.

SBD 46: Warning: Six-mile climb over Kramer Hills. Daylight Headlight Section continues.

South of Kramer Junction are the **Kramer Hills**. Pockets of gold were found in the hills in 1926 by brothers Ed and John Herkelrath. Soon a town boomed including a library and school. But when the ore was found to be low-grade and water so scarce, by 1931 the boom was over and the town abandoned. Another short-lived boom-bust was in 1885 when copper was discovered.

SBD 25: Note: End Daylight Headlight Section.

SBD 22: Adelanto comes from a Spanish word meaning "progress" or "advance." The town began in 1915 from the vision of E. H. Richardson, the inventor of an electric iron. Receiving a patent on his invention, Richardson sold the patent and bought land for $75,000, expecting to develop one of Southern California's first planned communities. He hoped to sell one-acre plots to WWI veterans with respiratory ailments and build a hospital especially for those with the disease. Unfortunately, his dream was never realized, but the town thrived anyway.

SBD 16: Look: WEST: **Rest Area** on **Air Base Road**. Also, Richardson Park with playground and picnic area, as well as Pryke Dog Park.

SBD 11: Look: EAST: Did you notice the cell-tree on steroids?

SBD 4: Note: End Daylight Headlight Section.

Note: I-15 North is accessible via the left lane.

Note: I-15 South is accessible via the right lane.

Enjoy the rest of your journey. Smooth roads and safe travels to you and yours. JBK

Alternate/Old US 395 Southbound

Alt WA 18: Intersection: <u>Right lane</u> to US 395 (both south and north) and N Lake Tahoe (via Mt. Rose Highway/SR 431). <u>Left lane</u> to Virginia City (National Historic Landmark via SR 341.) <u>Center lane</u> to Alternate/Old US 395 southbound.

Alt WA 16: Look: WEST: Did you notice the geothermal plants? These are part of the Steamboat Geothermal Power Complex. There are eight power plants. "Dry steam" is used to generate power directly from the steam generated inside the earth. The most common type of geothermal power plant is "flash steam," where water temperatures are more than 360°F.

Alt WA 16: Warning: Watch for wild horses on the road next seven miles.

Alt WA 16: Warning: Speed limit 50 mph.

Alt WA 16: Look: EAST: You may see steam rising from the hot springs. Nevada Historic Marker #198 **"Steamboat Springs"** explains:

> "These natural hot-springs are notable for their curative qualities. They were nationally acclaimed by President Ulysses S. Grant when he visited them in 1879.
>
> Early emigrants so named them, because of their puffing and blowing. Located in 1860 (by Felix Monet); a hospital, with adjacent bathhouses, was subsequently added by a Doctor Ellis (1861-1862).
>
> The Comstock mining activities and the coming of the Virginia and Truckee Railroad in 1871, caused Steamboat to became a terminal. Here materials for the silver mines were transferred to freight wagons for the steep haul to Virginia City. The completion of the tracks abolished the need for a junction, but its resort popularity was to reach its peak with the Bonanza Days.

To its "fine hotel, commodious dance-hall and elegant bar, came the legendary silver kings, politicos, gamblers and news chroniclers, escorting the lovely ladies of stage and opera house."

With borasca, attendance waned; fires destroyed the luxurious buildings, but the therapeutic waters remained, not only for health seekers, but for conditioning athletes - even producing mineral muds sought by cosmeticians and race horse owners."

State Historical Marker #198

Nevada State Park System & Daughters of the American Colonists Nevada Chapter

Note: The Mexican-Spanish definition of *borrasca* is unproductiveness, as in the mine was unproductive.

Alt WA 13: Look: What a great view of Mt. Rose-Ski Tahoe Area, Mount Rose Weather Observatory, and Galena Creek Bridge.

Mt. Rose-Ski Tahoe is 1,300 acres of groomed ski runs. Despite the name, the ski area is actually on the slopes of Slide Mountain rather than Mount Rose. At 8,260', the average yearly snowfall is 30'. But in 2017, a record 761" fell, that's more than double the average at nearly 64' of snow!

"Mount Rose Weather Observatory" is the location of Nevada State Historical Marker #230. It is the highest marker in the state at 8,900'. The marker explains the story best:

> "Two miles to the northwest of this point lies Mt. Rose. On the 10,778 foot summit, Dr. James Edward Church of the University of Nevada established one of America's first high-altitude meteorological observatories on June 29, 1905. At the observatory, he carried out his famed snow studies and developed the modern science of snow survey. Dr. Church's Nevada system of snow survey is used throughout the world today to predict seasonal water flow

from precipitation stored as snow pack. In his honor, the north summit of Mt. Rose has been named "Church Peak.""

When the observatory was originally built, it featured many designs that were unique or revolutionary for its time. The ability to record data without anyone being on site was one of them.

The **Galena Creek Bridge** is the world's longest cathedral arch bridge. It is 1,722' long, and the span of the arch is 689'. For an interesting article on the claim, _scan the QR Code in the Index of Websites_: **Galena Creek Bridge** and read Mark Robison's story.

Alt WA 12: Look: Locally this community is known as Pleasant Valley. It is at an elevation of 4,750'.

Alt WA 10: A: Camping: EAST on Eastlake Blvd. will take you to **Washoe Lake State Park** on the other side of Washoe Lake. _Scan the QR Code in the Index of Websites_: **Washoe Lake State Park** for more information.

Alt WA 10: Note: Begin Nevada Scenic Byway.

Alt WA 10: Entering **Washoe City**, elevation 5,035'. Founded in 1860 as a lumber camp for Virginia City, today Washoe City is considered a ghost town. In its heyday, Washoe City boasted a population of as many as 6,000 people. In 1861, it was the county seat. The streets were lined with restaurants, stores, saloons, livery stables, drugstores, bath houses and shaving emporiums. There were lawyers, doctors, and dentists. Later a school, churches, a hospital, a post office, and a courthouse and jail were built.

After the Virginia & Truckee Railroad was built, the population declined. Today fewer than 3,000 people live here. A decaying miner's cabin can be seen on the WEST side of the road protected by a chain-link fence.

A: Near here, EAST, is an E Clampus Vitus plaque that is on private property. It reads:

J. BUTLER KYLE

"Washoe City"

"During the early days of statehood Washoe City shone as a bright star in the new firmament"

Washoe City-Founded 1861-County Seat of Washoe County, Nevada territory. Timber supplier to the Comstock Lode. Home to 10 quartz mills and 281 stamps. Lost county seat to Reno 1871; victim of V&T Railroad success, Carson & Tahoe timbering and huge, new Carson river mills.

"By 1888... Nothing is left but ruins to mark the once thriving town."

Dedicated 17 Sept. 1977 by Snowshoe Thompson Chapter No. 1827

E Clampus Vitus & Dale L. Goings NGH

Alt WA 9: A: The **Chocolate Nugget Candy Factory** is a divine place to stop! The candy makers are "third generation and have been making quality candies and chocolates since 1936."

Outside the store is a short path to a giant miner statue. Owner Ed Feriance says, "He started out in Sparks, Nevada on top of the "Claims Stake Casino" in 1979. That casino only lasted about a year and he was then moved to the Nugget Casino in Reno. We moved him from the Nugget Casino to our Washoe Valley store in 1987. He's 35' tall and made out of fiberglass. Some say he was made from the image of Jack Longstreet the Nevada prospector. He was recently repainted in 2021 and continues to represent the Chocolate Nugget Candy Factory logo. You can visit him in Washoe Valley and get your picture with him." _Scan the QR Code in the Index of Websites_: **Chocolate Nugget Candy Factory** for more information.

Alt WA 8: Warning: Speed limit 45 mph. End of Nevada Scenic Byway.

NO EXIT NECESSARY: RENO, NV TO ADELANTO, CA

Alt WA 7: A: EAST: **Historic Winters Ranch House** and historic markers **"Winters Ranch."** Dedicated September 14, 1985 by Snowshoe Thomson Chapter No. 1827

E Clampus Vitus; and **"The Winters Ranch"** Nevada State Historic Marker #94. The house is #74001150 on the National Register of Historic Places.

"Winters Ranch"

"This is Rancho del Sierra, home of the Winters family from 1858 to 1953. The estate once covered six thousand acres of the surrounding property and included an orchard, horse race track and extensive livestock herds. The house was built by Theodore Winters, (circa 1862), who had become wealthy from part ownership in the Ophir Mine, located on the Comstock, which lies across the valley. The energetic lifestyle of the Winters family had a substantial impact on Nevada's social events, community services, and state politics."

"The Winters Ranch Rancho del Sierra"

"This large carpenter-gothic style structure, completed about 1864, was the ranch home of Theodore and Maggie Winters and their seven children. Originally this area was settled by Mormons, and the ranch was purchased from Mormons by Winters and his brother, from the proceeds of the Comstock. Theodore Winters immediately set out to enlarge his property and built the mansion you see. The ranch, at one time, consisted of around 6,000 acres.

Winters raised outstanding race horses; raced them here. He also had a large dairy operation; raised beef cattle, work horses and sheep.

Theodore Winters was active in politics, being elected territorial representative in 1862."

State Historical Marker No. 94

Nevada State Park System & Nevada Conservancy Association

Alt WA 7: Warning: Right lane only exit to I-580 northbound. Move left to exit onto I-580/US 395 Southbound or to continue on Alternate/Old US 395A southbound.

Alt WA 7: Warning: Speed limit 45 mph.

Alt WA 7: A: EAST: The **"Ophir Famous Mill Town"** monument was placed in 1961 by the Nevada Sagebrush Chapter, Daughters of the American Revolution.

> "Mill erected in 1861 for the reduction of the ore from famed Comstock Ophir Mine. The Ophir Mill ceased to operate in 1866 here a thriving town grew, second only in size to Washoe City, which at that time was the largest town in Washoe County."

Alt WA 6: A: WEST: **Davis Creek Regional Park**. Camping, hiking, and fishing are just a few of the recreation opportunity offered. *Scan the QR Code in the Index of Websites*: **Davis Creek Regional Park** for more information.

Alt WA 6: A: WEST: **A: Bowers Mansion Regional Park** offers a playground, seasonal outdoor pool, hiking trails, reservable picnic areas, horseshoe area, and tables/benches. *Scan the QR Code in the Index of Websites*: **Bowers Mansion Regional Park** for more information.

Bowers Mansion was built in 1863. For a brief but interesting article on the mansion, *scan the QR Code in the Index of Websites*: **Bowers Mansion history**. The Mansion and Park are two miles WEST off the exit. *Scan the QR Code in the Index of Websites*: **Bowers Mansion** for more information on the mansion and details of tours available. **Bowers Mansion Historic Marker #166** is at the south end of the park.

> "**Bowers Mansion** Built - 1864 Restored – 1967"

> "Bowers Mansion recalls the wealth of the Comstock Bonanza. Lemuel S. "Sandy" & Eilley Orrum Bowers were probably the first millionaires produced by the famous find in Gold Canyon. As

strangers, they had adjoining claims. After a rich vein was struck, they were soon married and had the mansion built.

Misfortune followed fortune and soon all was lost. The richness of their vein gave out, a new mill was destroyed, financiers balked, and then Sandy died in 1868. Maneuvering to make the property self sustaining, Eilley struggled on. Finally, in 1878, she lost the mansion by foreclosure to Myron C. Lake.

After that, the property had a succession of owners including Henry Ritter, who managed it as a popular resort from 1903 to 1946. Eilley Orrum Bowers died in poverty and unwittingly, she and Sandy left a legacy to Nevada."

State Historic Landmark No. 166

State Historic Preservation Office & Bowers Mansion Restoration Committee

Alt WA 6: Warning: Speed limit 55 mph.

Alt WA 4: A: EAST: Nevada Historic Marker #114 tells the brief history of **"Franktown."**

"Orson Hyde, probate judge of Carson County, Utah Territory, founded Franktown in the Wassau (Washoe) Valley in 1855.

A sawmill became an important enterprise in furnishing timber to the Comstock mines after 1859. The Dall Mill, a quartz mill of sixty stamps, employed hundreds of workers. Fertile farms surrounded the town.

With the completion of the railroad from Carson City to Virginia City in 1869, the milling business rapidly lost its importance and the once prosperous town declined."

State Historical Marker No. 114

J. BUTLER KYLE

State Historic Preservation Office

Alt WA 4: Look: WEST: Little evidence remains of the Little Valley Fire, other than the dead toothpick-looking snags lining the hillside. The fire ripped through Washoe Valley at 12:30 AM in the middle of the night of October 14, 2016, burning 2,291 acres and twenty-three homes, one owned by Bunny Ranch owner Dennis Hof. The fire was a direct result of Nevada Division of Forestry pulling crews off a prescribed burn after a high-wind forecast. The fire escaped when winds were 19 mph with gusts to 87 mph. *Scan the QR Code in the Index of Websites:* **Little Valley Fire** to read an interesting article about Dennis Hof and the fire.

Alt WA 3: Warning: Speed limit 50 mph.

Alt WA 2: A: Toiyabe Golf Club, WEST, is open to the public. For more information *scan the QR Code in the Index of Websites:* **Toiyabe Golf Club**.

Alt WA 2: Note: EAST on Bellevue Road returns to I-580/US 395, both southbound and northbound.

Alt WA 1: Note: Continuing straight will drop you back onto I-580/US 395 southbound. Turning left will take you to Washoe Lake State Park and New Washoe City via Eastlake Blvd. It will also return to I-580/US 395 northbound for Reno.

Alternate/Old US 395 Northbound

Alt WA 0: Note: Turning right (and then left at the stop sign) will ultimately take you back onto I-580/US 395 southbound. Turning left will take you to Washoe Lake State Park and New Washoe City via Eastlake Blvd, or a return to I-580/US 395 northbound for Reno.

Alt WA 0: Warning: Speed limit 45 mph.

Alt WA 1: Look: In the distance is Slide Mountain, recognizable by the slicked-off side of hillside. On Memorial Day 1983 part of the mountain slide off into the lakes below emptying them of hundreds of thousands of gallons of water and sending a 30' wall of mud and debris rushing down the Ophir Creek canyon and into Washoe Valley below. For a graphic collection of photographs of the disaster *scan the QR Code in the Index of Websites*: **Memorial Day 1983.**

Alt WA 1: Warning: Speed limit 50 mph.

Alt WA 2: A: Toiyabe Golf Club, WEST, is open to the public. For more information *scan the QR Code in the Index of Websites*: **Toiyabe Golf Club.**

Alt WA 2: Note: EAST on Bellevue Road returns to I-580/US 395 both south- and northbound.

Alt WA 3: Warning: Speed limit 55 mph.

Alt WA 3: Look: WEST: Little evidence remains of the Little Valley Fire, other than the dead toothpick-looking snags lining the hillside. The fire ripped through Washoe Valley at 12:30 AM in the middle of the night of October 14, 2016, burning 2,291 acres and twenty-three homes, one owned by Bunny Ranch owner Dennis Hof. The fire was a direct result of Nevada Division of Forestry pulling crews off a prescribed burn after a high-wind forecast. The fire escaped when winds were 19 mph with gusts to 87 mph. *Scan the QR Code in the Index of Websites*: **Little Valley Fire** to read an interesting article about Dennis Hof and the fire.

Alt WA 3: A: EAST: Nevada Historic Marker #114 tells the brief history of **"Franktown."**

"Orson Hyde, probate judge of Carson County, Utah Territory, founded Franktown in the Wassau (Washoe) Valley in 1855.

A sawmill became an important enterprise in furnishing timber to the Comstock mines after 1859. The Dall Mill, a quartz mill of sixty stamps, employed hundreds of workers. Fertile farms surrounded the town.

With the completion of the railroad from Carson City to Virginia City in 1869, the milling business rapidly lost its importance and the once prosperous town declined."

State Historical Marker No. 114

State Historic Preservation Office

Alt WA 4: Warning: Speed limit 45 mph.

Alt WA 6: A: WEST: **Bowers Mansion Regional Park** offers a playground, seasonal outdoor pool, hiking trails, reservable picnic areas, horseshoe area, and tables/benches. <u>Scan the QR Code in the Index of Websites</u>: **Bowers Mansion Regional Park** for more information.

Bowers Mansion was built in 1863. For a brief but interesting article on the mansion, <u>scan the QR Code in the Index of Websites</u>: **Bowers Mansion history.** The Mansion and Park are two miles WEST off the exit. <u>Scan the QR Code in the Index of Websites</u>: **Bowers Mansion** for more information on the mansion and details of tours available. **Bowers Mansion Historic Marker #166** is at the south end of the park.

"**Bowers Mansion** Built - 1864 Restored – 1967"

"Bowers Mansion recalls the wealth of the Comstock Bonanza. Lemuel S. "Sandy" & Eilley Orrum Bowers were probably the first millionaires produced by the famous find in Gold Canyon. As strangers, they had adjoining claims. After a rich vein was struck, they were soon married and had the mansion built.

Misfortune followed fortune and soon all was lost. The richness of their vein gave out, a new mill was destroyed, financiers balked, and then Sandy died in 1868. Maneuvering to make the property self sustaining, Eilley struggled on. Finally, in 1878, she lost the mansion by foreclosure to Myron C. Lake.

After that, the property had a succession of owners including Henry Ritter, who managed it as a popular resort from 1903 to 1946. Eilley Orrum Bowers died in poverty and unwittingly, she and Sandy left a legacy to Nevada."

State Historic Landmark No. 166

State Historic Preservation Office & Bowers Mansion Restoration Committee

Alt WA 6: A: EAST: The **"Ophir Famous Mill Town"** monument was placed in 1961 by the Nevada Sagebrush Chapter, Daughters of the American Revolution.

"Mill erected in 1861 for the reduction of the ore from famed Comstock Ophir Mine. The Ophir Mill ceased to operate in 1866 here a thriving town grew, second only in size to Washoe City, which at that time was the largest town in Washoe County."

Alt WA 7: A: WEST: **Davis Creek Regional Park**. Camping, hiking, and fishing are just a few of the recreation opportunity offered. *Scan the QR Code in the Index of Websites:* **Davis Creek Regional Park** for more information.

Alt WA 7: Warning: Intersection: Right turn to exit onto I-580/US 395 Southbound or continue straight on Alternate/Old US 395 to Reno. Left turn to exit to I-580 northbound.

J. BUTLER KYLE

Alt WA 7: Warning: Speed limit 45 mph. Begin Nevada Scenic Byway.

Alt WA 7: A: EAST: **Historic Winters Ranch House** and historic markers **"Winters Ranch"**, Dedicated September 14, 1985 by Snowshoe Thomson Chapter No. 1827

E Clampus Vitus; and **"The Winters Ranch"**, Nevada State Historic Marker #94. The house is #74001150 on the National Register of Historic Places.

"Winters Ranch"

"This is Rancho del Sierra, home of the Winters family from 1858 to 1953. The estate once covered six thousand acres of the surrounding property and included an orchard, horse race track and extensive livestock herds. The house was built by Theodore Winters, (circa 1862), who had become wealthy from part ownership in the Ophir Mine, located on the Comstock, which lies across the valley. The energetic lifestyle of the Winters family had a substantial impact on Nevada's social events, community services, and state politics."

"The Winters Ranch Rancho del Sierra"

"This large carpenter-gothic style structure, completed about 1864, was the ranch home of Theodore and Maggie Winters and their seven children. Originally this area was settled by Mormons, and the ranch was purchased from Mormons by Winters and his brother, from the proceeds of the Comstock. Theodore Winters immediately set out to enlarge his property and built the mansion you see. The ranch, at one time, consisted of around 6,000 acres.

Winters raised outstanding race horses; raced them here. He also had a large dairy operation; raised beef cattle, work horses and sheep.

Theodore Winters was active in politics, being elected territorial representative in 1862."

State Historical Marker No. 94

NO EXIT NECESSARY: RENO, NV TO ADELANTO, CA

Nevada State Park System & Nevada Conservancy Association

Alt WA 8: Warning: Speed limit 50 mph. Watch for wild horses on the road for next seven miles.

Alt WA 9: Entering **Washoe City**, elevation 5,035'. Founded in 1860 as a lumber camp for Virginia City, today Washoe City is considered a ghost town. In its heyday, Washoe City boasted a population of as many as 6,000 people. In 1861, it was the county seat. The streets were lined with restaurants, stores, saloons, livery stables, drugstores, bath houses and shaving emporiums. There were lawyers, doctors, and dentists. Later a school, churches, a hospital, a post office, and a courthouse and jail were built.

After the Virginia & Truckee Railroad was built, the population declined. Today fewer than 3,000 people live here. A decaying miner's cabin can be seen on the WEST side of the road protected by a chain-link fence.

A: Near here, EAST, is an E Clampus Vitus plaque that is on private property. It reads:

"Washoe City"

"During the early days of statehood Washoe City shone as a bright star in the new firmament"

Washoe City-Founded 1861-County Seat of Washoe County, Nevada territory. Timber supplier to the Comstock Lode. Home to 10 quartz mills and 281 stamps. Lost county seat to Reno 1871; victim of V&T Railroad success, Carson & Tahoe timbering and huge, new Carson river mills.

"By 1888... Nothing is left but ruins to mark the once thriving town."

Dedicated 17 Sept. 1977 by Snowshoe Thompson Chapter No. 1827

E Clampus Vitus & Dale L. Goings NGH

J. BUTLER KYLE

Alt WA 9: A: The **Chocolate Nugget Candy Factory** is a divine place to stop! The candy makers are "third generation and have been making quality candies and chocolates since 1936."

Outside the store is a short path to a giant miner statue. Owner Ed Feriance says, "He started out in Sparks, Nevada on top of the "Claims Stake Casino" in 1979. That casino only lasted about a year and he was then moved to the Nugget Casino in Reno. We moved him from the Nugget Casino to our Washoe Valley store in 1987. He's 35' tall and made out of fiberglass. Some say he was made from the image of Jack Longstreet the Nevada prospector. He was recently repainted in 2021 and continues to represent the Chocolate Nugget Candy Factory logo. You can visit him in Washoe Valley and get your picture with him." *Scan the QR Code in the Index of Websites*: **Chocolate Nugget Candy Factory** for more information.

Alt WA 10: Note: End Nevada Scenic Byway.

Alt WA 10: A: Camping: EAST on Eastlake Blvd. will take you to **Washoe Lake State Park** on the other side of Washoe Lake. *Scan the QR Code in the Index of Websites*: **Washoe Lake State Park** for more information.

Alt WA 10: Washoe Hill Memorial dedicated to victims of drunk driving. Elevation 5,089'.

Alt WA 11: Look: WEST: The **Galena Creek Bridge** is the world's longest cathedral arch bridge. It is 1,722" long, and the span of the arch is 689" feet. For an interesting article on the claim, *scan the QR Code in the Index of Websites*: **Galena Creek Bridge** and read Mark Robison's story.

Alt WA 12: Look: Locally, this community is known as Pleasant Valley. It is at an elevation of 4,750'.

Alt WA 16: Look: EAST: You may see steam rising from the hot springs. Nevada Historic Marker #198 **"Steamboat Springs"** explains:

NO EXIT NECESSARY: RENO, NV TO ADELANTO, CA

"These natural hot-springs are notable for their curative qualities. They were nationally acclaimed by President Ulysses S. Grant when he visited them in 1879.

Early emigrants so named them, because of their puffing and blowing. Located in 1860 (by Felix Monet); a hospital, with adjacent bathhouses, was subsequently added by a Doctor Ellis (1861-1862).

The Comstock mining activities and the coming of the Virginia and Truckee Railroad in 1871, caused Steamboat to became a terminal. Here materials for the silver mines were transferred to freight wagons for the steep haul to Virginia City. The completion of the tracks abolished the need for a junction, but its resort popularity was to reach its peak with the Bonanza Days.

To its "fine hotel, commodious dance-hall and elegant bar, came the legendary silver kings, politicos, gamblers and news chroniclers, escorting the lovely ladies of stage and opera house."

With borasca, attendance waned; fires destroyed the luxurious buildings, but the therapeutic waters remained, not only for health seekers, but for conditioning athletes - even producing mineral muds sought by cosmeticians and race horse owners."

State Historical Marker #198

Nevada State Park System & Daughters of the American Colonists Nevada Chapter

Note: The Mexican-Spanish definition of *borrasca* is unproductiveness, as in the mine was unproductive.

Alt WA 16: Look: WEST: Did you notice the geothermal plants? These are part of the Steamboat Geothermal Power Complex. There are eight power plants. "Dry steam" is used to generate power directly from the steam generated inside the earth. The most common type of geothermal power plant is "flash steam", where water temperatures are more than 360°F.

Alt WA 18: Intersection: <u>Left lane</u> to US 395 (both south and north) and N Lake Tahoe (via Mt. Rose Highway/SR 431). <u>Right lane</u> to Virginia City (National Historic Landmark via SR 341.) <u>Center lane</u> to Virginia Street and northbound onramp to US 395.

US 395 Business Route (Carson City) Southbound

CC 9: Exit 8 – **US 395 Business Route** to Carson Street, West Side Historic District, and Carson Tahoe Regional Medical Center Hospital. This route reconnects in six miles with US 395 southbound or a return to I-580/US 395 northbound.

Warning: Exit 8 is an 8% downgrade. Speed limit 45 mph.

Note: Carson City has forty-seven Electric Vehicle Charging Stations. *Scan the QR Code in the Index of Websites*: **EV Stations - Carson City** for a link to a map of their locations.

Mile 6: WEST on Medical Parkway to hospital – **Carson Tahoe Regional Medical Center**.

Mile 5: A: WEST: **Silver Oak Golf and Event Center** is a public golf course spread over 150 acres in the western foothills of Carson City. *Scan the QR Code in the Index of Websites*:

Silver Oak Golf for more information.

Mile 4: Warning: Speed limit 35 mph. Trucks use left lane next two miles.

Mile 4: Turn EAST for Fallon on Williams St./US 50.

Mile 4: Warning: Lane reduction to two lanes and 25 mph through Nevada Historic District and past the State Capital, Historic markers, the Nevada State Museum, and State Legislature are all in this area.

Mile 3: A: WEST are two monuments. On the side of the historic St. Charles Hotel is a plaque placed by E Clampus Vitus Snowshoe Thomson Chapter #1827 "**St. Charles Hotel.**" In the plaza is monument "**In Search Of The Pony Express Station Marker.**" *Scan the QR Code in the Index of Websites*: **E Clampus Vitus** for other historic markers around Carson City and the area.

J. BUTLER KYLE

"St. Charles Hotel"

"One of the oldest continuously operating hotels in the state. It is composed of two hotels. The three story St. Charles and the two story Muller House next door south. Construction of both buildings took place in 1862 with completion in August of that year. Geo. Remington, Al Muller Dan Plitt were the first proprietors. In September, Charlie Slicer became the first bar owner serving the finest spirits that money could buy. As one of the most elegant hotels in the state it became the main stage stop in Carson City. The Best known and most popular owner was George Tufly, a banker and man about town, who had it from 1866 to 1875. It has had many other owners. Since. It is currently listed in the National Register of Historic Places of the United States."

Dedicated This 215th Day of August 5989 by the Snowshoe Thomson Chapter #1827 of the Ancient and Honourable Order of E Clampus Vitus.

"In Search Of The Pony Express"

"Dedicated April 12, 1996 Carson City Original Station Apr 3, 1860 – Nov 20, 1861

By Ron L. & Peggy Clark & Family, Bob & Tina McFadden, Mae & Jim Thorpe, The Bike Smith, Betty Young & Erica Young, Pony Express Trail Association"

Mile 2: A: WEST just past the roundabout is Nevada Historic Marker #184 **"Gardner's Ranch"** and **Toiyabe National Forest Carson Ranger Station.**

"On this site in the period from 1870 until 1918 stood the ornate, two-story home of Matthew Culbertson Gardner, rancher and lumberman. The residence was headquarters for Gardner's 300 acre ranch in meadows to the southward.

Here was located, 1870-1898, the Carson-Tahoe Lumber and Fluming Company's large lumberyard. During the 1870's and 1880's, Gardner logged south of Lake Tahoe for the company and built the only standard gauge logging railroad in the Tahoe Basin. He maintained his home here.

Gardner died in 1908. The residence was destroyed by a fire August 20, 1918. Many of the old trees on the ground once shaded the Gardner family."

State Historical Marker No. 184

Nevada State Park System & Carson City Historical Commission

Mile 2: A: EAST, at the very next turn in to the small mall, back behind the first building on the edge of the little park is Nevada Historic Marker #193 **"Historic Flume and Lumberyard."**

"Approximately one-half mile south of this point and west of the present highway lay the immense lumberyard of the Carson-Tahoe Lumber and Fluming Company, the greatest of the Comstock lumbering combines operating in the Lake Tahoe Basin during 1870-1898.

Situated at the terminus of the 12 mile "V" flume from Spooners Summit in the Sierra Nevada, the lumberyard was approximately one mile long and one-half mile wide. A spur line of the Virginia and Truckee Railroad served the lumberyard. The spur ran adjacent to this site and carried rough lumber to the company's planing mill and box factory, one-half mile north on Stewart Street. It also carried timbers and cordwood to the Carson Yards to be hauled to the Comstock mines and mills."

State Historic Marker No. 193

Nevada State Park System & Carson City Historical Commission

Mile 1: Warning: Speed limit 35 mph.

Mile 1: A: Carson City Chamber of Commerce and **Nevada State Railroad Museum** are both located here. *Scan the QR Code in the Index of Websites*: **Carson City Chamber of Commerce** for information on the city. *Scan the QR Code in the Index of Websites*: **Nevada State Railroad Museum** for information on the railroad and tour times.

Mile 0: Warning: Intersection: Right lane to Lake Tahoe via US 50 West over Spooner Summit. Center lane continues US 395 to Minden/Gardnerville and points south. Left lane to

I-580/US 395 for Reno, northbound.

US 395 Business Route (Carson City) Northbound

Note: US 395 Business Route to Carson Street, West Side Historic District, and Carson Tahoe Regional Medical Center Hospital. This route reconnects in six miles with I-580/US 395 northbound.

Mile 0: Warning: Speed limit 35 mph. Three-lanes transition to two. To continue north on Business Route US 395, keep left.

Note: Carson City has forty-seven **Electric Vehicle Charging Stations**. *Scan the QR Code in the Index of Websites*: **EV Stations - Carson City** for a link to a map of their locations.

Mile 1: A: EAST on Snyder Avenue are three Nevada Historic Markers – #76 Eagle Valley, #77 Dat-So-La-Lee, and #91 Stewart Indian School, as well as Stewart Indian School, a National Historic Register of Places.

Mile 2: A: Carson City Chamber of Commerce and **Nevada State Railroad Museum** are both located here. *Scan the QR Code in the Index of Websites*: **Carson City Chamber of Commerce** for information on the city. *Scan the QR Code in the Index of Websites*: **Nevada State Railroad Museum** for information on the railroad and tour times.

Mile 2: A: EAST, just past the stoplight at Fairview, turn in to the small mall, back behind the first building on the edge of the little park is Nevada Historic Marker #193 **"Historic Flume and Lumberyard."**

> "Approximately one-half mile south of this point and west of the present highway lay the immense lumberyard of the Carson-Tahoe Lumber and Fluming Company, the greatest of the Comstock lumbering combines operating in the Lake Tahoe Basin during 1870-1898.

J. BUTLER KYLE

Situated at the terminus of the 12 mile "V" flume from Spooners Summit in the Sierra Nevada, the lumberyard was approximately one mile long and one-half mile wide. A spur line of the Virginia and Truckee Railroad served the lumberyard. The spur ran adjacent to this site and carried rough lumber to the company's planing mill and box factory, one-half mile north on Stewart Street. It also carried timbers and cordwood to the Carson Yards to be hauled to the Comstock mines and mills."

State Historic Marker No. 193

Nevada State Park System & Carson City Historical Commission

Mile 2: A: WEST just before the roundabout is Nevada Historic Marker #184 **"Gardner's Ranch"** and Toiyabe National Forest Carson Ranger Station.

"On this site in the period from 1870 until 1918 stood the ornate, two-story home of Matthew Culbertson Gardner, rancher and lumberman. The residence was headquarters for Gardner's 300 acre ranch in meadows to the southward.

Here was located, 1870-1898, the Carson-Tahoe Lumber and Fluming Company's large lumberyard. During the 1870's and 1880's, Gardner logged south of Lake Tahoe for the company and built the only standard gauge logging railroad in the Tahoe Basin. He maintained his home here.

Gardner died in 1908. The residence was destroyed by a fire August 20, 1918. Many of the old trees on the ground once shaded the Gardner family."

State Historical Marker No. 184

Nevada State Park System & Carson City Historical Commission

NO EXIT NECESSARY: RENO, NV TO ADELANTO, CA

Mile 4: Warning: Lane reduction to two lanes and 25 mph through Nevada Historic District and past the State Capital. Historic markers, the Nevada State Museum, Federal Building, State Legislature and Assembly are all in this area.

Mile 4: Turn EAST for Fallon on Williams St./US 50 East.

Mile 4: Warning: Speed limit 35 mph.

Mile 5: A: WEST: **Silver Oak Golf and Event Center** is a public golf course spread over one hundred fifty acres in the western foothills of Carson City. *Scan the QR Code in the Index of Websites:* **Silver Oak Golf** for more information.

Mile 6: WEST on Medical Parkway to hospital – Carson Tahoe Regional Medical Center.

Mile 6: Continue straight to I-580/US 395 northbound. **Warning:** The onramp is a 7% climb to the top of the hill.

J. BUTLER KYLE

Index
Nevada Index

Nevada Facts and Trivia

Nevada Index of Attractions

Bently Heritage Trail DO29

California Trail Crossing WA 41, WA 22, DO 31

Carson City Chamber of Commerce MILE 1

Chocolate Nugget Candy Factory WA 8

Countess Angela Dandini Gardens WA 31

Desert Research Institute WA 31

Genoa, Town of DO 33, DO 26

Johnson Lane OHV Access DO 27

Lahontan National Fish Hatchery Complex DO 17

Marsha's Park DO 24

Nevada State Railroad Museum MILE 1

Pony Express Crossing CC 5

Sierra Nevada Zoological Park WA 39

Silver Oak Golf and Event Center MILE 5

Sunridge Golf and Recreations DO 33, DO 32

Toiyabe Golf Club WA 3

Topaz Lodge DO 2

Wildlife Viewing Area (Carson River) DO 16

Nevada Index of Camping and Day Use Parks

Bowers Mansion Regional Park WA 8

Davis Creek Regional Park WA 8

Topaz Lake Recreation Area DO 2

Washoe Lake State Park WA 8

Nevada Index of Cities

Carson City CC9

Cold Springs WA 39

Gardnerville DO 23

Golden Valley WA 31

Holbrook Junction DO 4

Lemmon Valley WA 32

Minden DO 24

Reno WA 24

Stead WA 34

Nevada Index of Counties

Carson City CC 9

Douglas DO 33

Washoe WA 41

Nevada Index of Historical Markers and Monuments

Birthplace of Nevada #12 DO 26

Bowers Mansion #166 WA 8

Cradlebaugh Bridge #123 DO 30

Double Springs #126 DO 8

Dresslerville #131 DO 18

Franktown #114 Alt WA 4

Gardner's Ranch #184 MILE 2

Gardnerville #129 DO 23

Historic Flume and Lumberyard #193 MILE 2

Historic Transportation #256 WA 39

Minden #130 DO 24

St. Charles Hotel MILE 3

Steamboat Springs Alt WA 16

Twelve Mile House #125 DO 18

The Winters Ranch #94 Alt WA 7

Washoe City Alt WA 10

Winters Ranch Alt WA 7

Nevada Index of Lakes, Rivers, and Water Sheds

Topaz Lake DO 2

Walker River Water Shed DO 7

Washoe Lake WA 7

Nevada Index of Mountains and Summits

Pine Nut Mountains DO 27

Simee Dimeh Summit DO10

Nevada Index of Ranger Stations

Toiyabe National Forest Carson Ranger Station MILE 2

Nevada Index of Native American Information

Washoe Tribe of Nevada and California (Wa She Shu) DO 19

Nevada Index of Roads

Alternate/Old US 395 Southbound ALT WA 18, ALT WA 6

Alternate/Old US 395 Northbound ALT WA 0

Interstate 580 (I-580)

SR 207 (Lake Tahoe via Kingsbury Grade) DO 25

SR 208 (alternate route to Bishop, CA) DO 4

SR 431 (Mount Rose Highway) WA 13

US 50 (Lake Tahoe via Spooner Summit) CC 1

US 395 Business Route CC 9, CC 1

US Route 395 (US 395) WA 1

California Index

California Facts and Trivia

California Index of Attractions

Bodie State Historic Park MNO 71

Bristlecone Pine Information INY 101

California Trail Crossing MNO 110

Cottonwood Charcoal Kilns INY 45

Crowley Lake Columns MNO 19

Eastern California Museum INY 74

Eastern Sierra Visitor Center INY 55

English pedunculate Oak tree INY 58

Fales Hot Springs MNO 90

Fossil Falls INY 13

Grave of 1872 Earthquake Victims INY 59

June Lake Scenic Loop MNO 47, MNO 40

Keogh Hot Springs INY 108

Lone Pine Film History Museum INY 58

Lower Owens River Project INY 82

Manzanar National Historic Site INY 68

Mammoth Lake Scenic Loop MNO 31, MNO 26

Mono Basin Interpretive Center MNO 52

Mono Basin Museum MNO 52

Mono Lake Boardwalk MNO 53

Mono Lake Cemetery MNO 56

Mono Lake Park Nature Trail MNO 56

Mono Lake Overlook MNO 51

Mono Lake South Tufa Self-Guided Nature Trail MNO 46

Mono Lake Vista Point MNO 63

Mt. Whitney Fish Hatchery INY 76

Obsidian Dome Road MNO 37

Old School House Museum MNO 52

Owens Valley Paiute Shoshone Cultural Center INY 116

Southern Inyo Museum INY 58

Topaz Agriculture Inspection Station MNO 120

Tinemahah Wildlife Viewing Area INY 93

Uniroyal Girl INY 0

Upside-Down House MNO 52

Wheeler Guard Station MNO 92

Wildlife Viewing Area (Tule Elk) INY 93

California Index of Camping and Day Use Parks

Chris Flat Seasonal Campground MNO 97

Crowley Lake BLM Campground MNO 18

Diaz Lake Campground INY 55

Glacier View Campground INY 101

Goodale Creek Campground INY 87

Hartley Springs Campground MNO 37

Millpond Campground INY 121

Obsidian Campground MNO 93

Shingle Mill Flat Day Use Park MNO 101

Taboose Creek Campground INY 88

Tuff Campground MNO 11

California Index of Cities

Adelanto SBD 22

Big Pine INY 101

Bishop INY 119

Bridgeport MNO 76

Cartago INY 37

Coleville MNO 112

Dunmovin INY 21

Grant INY 33

Independence INY 74

Inyokern KER 24

Johannesburg KER 0

Kramer Junction SBD 46

Lee Vining MNO 52

Lone Pine INY 58

Olancha INY 35

Pearsonville INY 0

Randsburg KER 1

Red Mountain SBD 72

Ridgecrest INY 17

J. BUTLER KYLE

Tom's Place MNO 11

Topaz MNO 117

Walker MNO 108

California Index of Counties

Inyo INY 130

Kern KER 37

Mono MNO 120

San Bernardino SBD 73

California Index of Deserts, Mountains, and Summits

———

Conway Summit MNO 63

Deadman Summit MNO 36

Devil's Gate Summit MNO 88

El Paso Mountains KER 24

Inyo Mountains INY 101

Kramer Hills SBD 46

Mojave Desert KER 24

Mono-Inyo Craters MNO 50

Sherwin Summit MNO 8

Sierra Nevada Mountains MNO 120

Sweetwater Mountains MNO 94

White Mountains MNO 8

California Index of Historical Markers and Monuments

The Alabama Gates INY 64

Avalanche 1911 MNO 59

Boom and Bust MNO 70

Cartago Boat Landing INY 37

Casa Diablo MNO 26

Charcoal Cottonwood Kilns INY 45

Charley's Butte INY 89

Disaster in 1872 INY 59

Dog Town 1857 MNO 70

Edge of a Dream MNO 70

El Camino Sierra INY 109

Farley's Olancha Mill INY 34

Fremont's Trail 1844 MNO 88

From Trail to Highway INY 109

Grave of Adeline Carson Stilts MNO 56

Historic Atolia and the Stringer District SBD 69

Historic Silver Dollar Saloon SBD 72

James D. Birchim INY 116

Lee Vining MNO 52

Legend of Deadman MNO 34

Little Bodie MNO 68

Lost Cement Mine MNO 33

Lynching of the Convicts INY 119

March 26, 1988 INY 59

McGee Mountain Rope Tow #34 MNO 18

Mono Diggin's MNO 63

Mono Lake ...? MNO 51

Mono Lake & Hollywood MNO 51

Mono Lake – Lake of Many Uses MNO 51

Old Highway 23 INY 109

Pine Creek Mine INY 129

Poor Farm MNO 72

Santa Fe Silver Mine SBD 72

T-130 and Crew MNO 108

Tule Elk INY 93

Westgaard Pass Toll Road INY 101

California Index of Lakes, Rivers, and Reservoirs

Bridgeport Reservoir MNO 75

Crowley Lake MNO 19

Diaz Lake INY 55

Haiwee Reservoir INY 24

Little Lake INY 11

Mono Lake MNO 52

Owens Lake INY 42

Owens River INY 84

Owens River Gorge INY 84

Tinemaha Reservoir INY 93

West Walker River MNO 103

California Index of National Forest and Wilderness, and Ranger Stations

Bridgeport Ranger Station MNO 75

Humboldt-Toiyabe National Forest MNO 101

Inyo National Forest MNO 44

John Muir Wilderness MNO 21

Mono Basin National Forest MNO 59

California Index of Native American Information

Big Pine Band of Owens Valley Paiute Shoshone Indians of the Big Pine Reservation

Bishop Paiute Tribe INY 101

Fort Independence Reservation INY 77

Lone Pine Paiute-Shoshone Reservation INY 58

California Index of Rest Areas

Air Base Road SBD 16

Coso Junction Rest Area INY 18

County Park and Rest Area on Hackney Drive MNO 108

Crestview Rest Area MNO 33

Division Creek Rest Area INY 84

Independence County Park and Rest Area INY 74

California Index of Roads

CA 89 (Monitor Pass) MNO 118

CA 108 (Sonora Pass) MNO 94

CA 120 (Tioga Pass) MNO 51

CA 167 (Hawthorne, Nevada) MNO 58

CA 168 (Ancient Bristlecone Pine Forest) INY 101

Eastern Sierra Scenic Byway - Begin MNO 106, End INY 10

Grand Army of the Republic Highway INY 109

US 6 (alternate route from Holbrook Junction, Nevada to Bishop, California) INY 116

J. BUTLER KYLE

Index of QR Codes for Websites and Other Links

Alternative Fuels Corridor

https://tinyurl.com/alternativefuelscorridor

Bently Heritage Trail

Bishop Chamber of Commerce

Bowers Mansion

Bowers Mansion History

Bowers Mansion Historic Marker #166

Bowers Mansion Regional Park

California Trail Auto Tour Route

California Trail Crossing

NO EXIT NECESSARY: RENO, NV TO ADELANTO, CA

Campgrounds:

Chris Flat Campground

Crowley Lake Campground

Davis Creek Regional Park

Diaz Lake Campground

Glacier View Campground

Goodale Creek Campground

Hartley Springs Campground

Millpond Campground

Obsidian Campground

NO EXIT NECESSARY: RENO, NV TO ADELANTO, CA

Taboose Creek Campground

Topaz Lake Recreation Area

Tuff Campground

Washoe Lake State Park

Carson City Chamber of Commerce

Chocolate Nugget Candy Factory

Coldcock Whiskey

Crowley Lake Columns

NO EXIT NECESSARY: RENO, NV TO ADELANTO, CA

E Clampus Vitus Snowshoe Thompson

Electric Vehicle Charging Stations

Carson City

Minden/Gardnerville

Reno

Fossil Falls

Galena Creek Bridge

Ghost Towns – Cartago, Grant, Johannesburg, Olancha

Inyokern Airport and Pistachio controversy

Johnson Lane OHV

https://tinyurl.com/JohnsonLaneOHV

NO EXIT NECESSARY: RENO, NV TO ADELANTO, CA

Joshua trees and funky statues

Little Valley Fire

Lone Pine Film History Museum

Mark Twain

Memorial Day 1983

Mono County autumn colors guide & map

Mono Lake South Tufa Self-Guided Nature Trail

Nevada State Railroad Museum

NO EXIT NECESSARY: RENO, NV TO ADELANTO, CA

Owens Lake and surrounding area

Owens Lake Sea Monster Tale

Owens Valley History

Owl Spy Shop

Pearsonville

Piper vs. Big Pine

Pony Express Trail Crossing

Randsburg Desert Museum

NO EXIT NECESSARY: RENO, NV TO ADELANTO, CA

Silver Oak Golf and Event Center

Sunridge Golf and Recreations

Toiyabe Golf Club

Uniroyal Girl

US 6 – Grand Army of the Republic

Yosemite Reservations

References

California tidbits

https://sites.google.com/site/caplacesofinterest/50-facts-and-tidbits

El Camino Sierra – Inyo County

https://inyocountyvisitor.com/el-camino-sierra/

Historic markers and National Registry of Historic Places

https://noehill.com/

"Lunch Break" Review from *Tripadvisor.com*. Used with permission.

Nevada tidbits

https://www.50states.com/facts/nevada.htm

Steamboat Geothermal Power Complex

https://www.renolocalnv.com/Reno/Steam-Plant/

<u>**Wikipedia Research**</u>:

Alice Piper, Big Pine, California

Cities and Towns – Nevada: Carson City, Gardnerville, Minden, Reno, Stead

Cities and Towns – California: Adelanto, Big Pine, Bishop, Bridgeport, Cartago, Coleville, Dunmovin, Grant, Independence, Inyokern, Johannesburg, Kramer Junction, Lee Vining, Lone Pine, Olancha, Pearsonville, Randsburg, Red Mountain, Tom's Place, Topaz, Walker

Counties – Nevada: Douglas, Washoe

Counties – California: Mono, Inyo, Kern, San Bernardino

J. BUTLER KYLE

Lakes – Nevada: Topaz, Washoe

Lakes and Rivers – California:

Bridgeport Reservoir, Convict Lake, Crowley Lake, Haiwee Reservoir, Little Lake, Mono Lake, Owens River Gorge, Tinemaha Reservoir, West Walker River

Mountains and Desert: El Paso Mountains, Inyo Mountains, Kramer Hills, Mojave Desert, Sierra Nevada, Sweetwater Mountains, White Mountains

National Forests and Wilderness: John Muir Wilderness, Mono Basin NF, Inyo NF

Native American: Bishop Paiute Tribe, Lone Pine Paiute-Shoshone Reservation

Norman Clyde, Big Pine, California

Other: Bodie State Historic Park, Fales Hot Springs, Fossil Falls, Inyokern Airport, Joshua Tree, Manzanar National Historic Site, Owens Valley Radio Observatory, Wheeler Guard Station

Roads: Grand Army of the Republic Highway, Interstate 580, State Route 431, US Highway 395

Summits: Conway Summit, Simee Dimeh Summit

Trail Crossings: California Trail, Pony Express

About the Author

J. Butler Kyle has thousands and thousands of hours traveling America's roads with her husband as they crisscrossed the US. All the way pouring over maps and reading aloud the local history and flavor of the country they were seeing, researching things to see and do along the route.

They have lived in over one hundred places in the US, including an island in the Gulf of Alaska. Twenty-four years were in some form of an RV. All those locations were aviation related, including aerial firefighting while J. was Crew Chief on a Single Engine Air Tanker (SEAT).

J. has written other travel and visitor guides (Prince of Wales Island, Alaska); humorous short stories for *Aviation USA* and *RV Life*; expanded the Southeast Alaska portion of *The Milepost*; and ghost-written three memoirs. Her first self-published book, *Tales From the Dockside*, is a collection of fun and often embarrassing vignettes of her and her husband's two years living on a boat in the Gulf of Alaska.

Northern Nevada is where J. calls home with said husband, their family of kitties, and whatever strays wander in. She loves to garden, capture photographs, and of course travel. J. once helped evacuate a casino of all its cash, but that's another story.

You can reach J. at jbutlerkyle@yahoo.com, visit her website at jbutlerkyle.com, or find her on Facebook at J. Butler Kyle, Scribe.

Read more at https://jbutlerkyle.com/.

www.ingramcontent.com/pod-product-compliance
Lightning Source LLC
LaVergne TN
LVHW011417080426
835512LV00005B/114